THE BAG APRON: THE POET
AND HIS COMMUNITY

The Bag Apron: The Poet and his Community

John Montague

A collaboration between the

THE IRELAND CHAIR OF POETRY

and

UNIVERSITY COLLEGE DUBLIN PRESS

Preas Choláiste Ollscoile Bhaile Átha Cliath

2017

First published 2017
UNIVERSITY COLLEGE DUBLIN PRESS
UCD Humanities Institute
Room H103
Belfield
Dublin 4
www.ucdpress.ie

'The Bag Apron or The Poet and His Community',
'Short Thoughts on the Long Poem' and 'The
Challenge of Translation' were originally published
in *The Poet's Chair: The First Nine Years of the Ireland
Chair of Poetry* (The Lilliput Press, 2008), and are
reproduced by kind permission of the publisher.

'Samuel Beckett, Neighbour' was originally
published in John Montague, Company: *A
Chosen Life* (Duckworth, 2001), and is
reproduced here by kind permission of the
publisher.

ISBN 978-1-910820-16-2
ISSN 2009-8065 The Poet's Chair Series

CIP data available from the British Library

The right of John Montague to be identified as the
author of this work has been asserted by him

Typeset in Adobe Kepler by Ryan Shiels
Text design by Lyn Davies Design
Printed in England on acid-free paper
by Antony Rowe, Chippenham, Wiltshire

Contents

vii   FOREWORD

ix   PREFACE BY SEAMUS HEANEY

1   The Bag Apron or The Poet
         and His Community

15   Short Thoughts on the Long
         Poem

25   The Challenge of Translation

35   Samuel Beckett, Neighbour

61   BIOGRAPHICAL NOTE

62   ACKNOWLEDGEMENTS

63   BIBLIOGRAPHY

65   AFTERWORD

FOREWORD

The Trustees of the Ireland Chair of Poetry, in collaboration with UCD Press, are delighted to republish the lectures of John Montague in this handsome volume. The annual lectures of the first three distinguished poets to hold the Chair, John Montague, Nuala Ní Dhomhnaill and Paul Durcan, were originally published in a joint volume, *The Poet's Chair*, by Lilliput Press in 2008. Since then, UCD Press, in the series Writings from the Ireland Chair of Poetry, has published the lectures of the three eminent poets who subsequently held the Chair: Michael Longley, Harry Clifton and Paula Meehan. This series of individual volumes is now being enhanced with the republication of the lectures of the first three professors; we are most grateful to Lilliput Press for their immediate consent and their help with this project.

The Ireland Chair of Poetry was established to honour Seamus Heaney's Nobel Prize for Literature in 1995. Modelled on the Oxford Chair of Poetry which Seamus held with grace and distinction, the Ireland Chair is a cross-border collaboration involving the two Irish Arts Councils, north and south, Queen's University Belfast, Trinity College Dublin and University College Dublin. A highlight of the professorship is the annual public lecture each professor gives and their publication constitutes an important record of the poets' engagement with their own work and that of other poets. Each of them has carried on a noble tradition of sharing their learning with new generations.

As Donnell Deeny noted in his Preface to the original publication of these lectures, John Montague's "œuvre marks him out as a poet of the first rank. He is a critic and prose writer of achievement. He is of the island as a whole and of its exiles." It was with great sorrow that the Trustees learned of his death in Nice in December 2016. We are most grateful to his widow, Elizabeth Wassell, for her help with this volume.

Our sincere thanks to Mary Clayton who worked tirelessly to bring this project to fruition. I must also thank all of my other fellow Trustees, both former and currently serving, ably supported by administrator Niamh McCabe. The Ireland Chair of Poetry Trust has an assured future because of their commitment and I know that each one of them would say, with me, that it is an honour to be associated with such a visionary project.

SHEILA PRATSCHKE
Chair of the Board of Trustees, Ireland Chair of Poetry
September 2017

PREFACE BY SEAMUS HEANEY

Remarks on the occasion of John Montague's appointment to the post of Ireland Professorship of Poetry, 14 May 1998

The Ireland Professorship of Poetry is an honour as well as an office. To hold this Professorship is to stand as a representative of the art within the Irish university system. The post is intended to manifest the value of poetry within our cultural and intellectual life, north and south – and nobody is better fitted to do this job than John Montague. In the course of a lifetime, his fidelity to his vocation and his fulfilment of its public demands have been ready, steady and characteristically vigorous.

I was proud to be associated with the establishment of the Chair and delighted with the outcome of this first appointment – an appointment, it must be said, regarded with the utmost seriousness by the universities concerned. They liaised and debated, evolved a job description, a well-ordered appointments procedure and have managed to agree upon certain services that will be required from the holder of the post.

The Arts Councils, north and south, were also crucial to the inception of the scheme and to the maintenance of momentum. They and their officers were aware of the complexity and challenge of what they were taking on, but did not flinch at the difficulties. They knew that when it comes to making decisions and judgements about poets and poetry in contemporary Ireland, you need the wisdom of Solomon and the decisiveness, if not the ruthlessness, of Procrustes – and it also helps to have the sanity of a Portia and a bit of the recklessness of King Lear. But one feature of the process deserves special mention: not only is the successful candidate informed ahead of time, but other poets on the short list are also made aware of the decision and are thus spared the indignity of discovering their un-success in public at the official announcement ceremony. That embarrassment, unfortunately, is too often the penalty of being short-listed for some other important literary awards in Ireland and in Britain. In this case, however, the poets concerned were informed privately of their candidacy and of their standing after the final, very difficult decision had been taken.

In the end, John Montague's name prevailed and it is a pleasure for me to make the formal announcement of his appointment. What we are honouring is not only John's achievement as a poet: equally important on this occasion is his critical acuity about poetry in Irish and English; his long and passionate involvement with the land of Ireland, north and south; his concern with the significance of its landmarks and the meaning of its place names, from the Glen of the Hazels in Tyrone to Mount Eagle in Kerry. Nor should we overlook his experience as a teacher in universities in France and Ireland and the United States, his international standing in the world of letters, his record as an active witness and committed participant at those moments of historical crisis that have marked each and every one of us. All of which makes John Montague an ideal first appointment to this uniquely important office.

I began to read John's poetry in what was for me the *annus mirabilis* of 1962–63, the year when I came alive to the excitement of reading contemporary Irish and British poetry and yielded to the desire to write poems of my own – a desire that both ravishes and frustrates at the same time. I felt an almost literal quickening in my bones as I read for the first time poems that brought me to my senses in a new way, poems that would stay with me for a lifetime, such as Patrick Kavanagh's *The Great Hunger*, Ted Hughes's 'The Thought Fox' and 'View of a Pig', R.S. Thomas's 'Evans' and 'Iago Prytherch', and John Montague's 'The Water Carrier' and 'Like Dolmens round my Childhood, the Old People'. John Montague's essays and reviews were also appearing in those years, helping to establish a home-based critical idiom that was bracing and clarifying – as in his important early review essay (in *Poetry Ireland*) on the poetry of John Hewitt, and his reappropriation in the famous *Dolmen Miscellany of Irish Writing* of Goldsmith's 'The Deserted Village' as an Irish poem. Here was somebody sketching out a way of 'bringing it all back home', prefiguring the Hibernocentric reading of Anglo-Irish literature upon which academic critics would be engaged for decades to come.

This was also when I first met John in person, under the sponsoring eye of Mary and Pearse O'Malley in their house on Derryvolgie Avenue, and felt the reach of that long bony arm across my shoulder, and felt also the test and flush of his giddy, goading intelligence. Ten years older, farther travelled, more widely published, he arrived on the scene like a combination of talent scout and poetic DI, a kind of government inspector from the government of tongue sent in by the *aos dána* of the day, that body of unacknowledged legislators legislating for all they were worth from Monaghan to MacDaids, from rue Daguerre to Baggot Street Deserta. But there is no need to wax nostalgic about those days: they generated intensity and energy and edge, a combination of circumstances that has continued through the decades and done us all good as individual poets. In the course of the past few months, therefore, it has been a moving and confirming experience for me to re-read John's era-defining collections and to re-encounter them in the magnificent *Collected Poems* – so admirably produced by The Gallery Press. Here is an œuvre that inheres in and extends the tradition of Irish poetry – a tradition that began with the magical invocations of the *ur*-poet Amergin and was reconstituted for our time by the transformative vision of W. B. Yeats.

For many of us, Montague's poems and individual lines from his poems have attained 'that dark permanence of ancient forms', forms which shadowed his own imagination as he grew up in Garvaghey. It was there he became aware of 'lines of history, lines of power' in 'the rough field of the universe', aware of 'the sound a wound makes', of the stress of violence. But there too he became capable of surmounting 'all legendary obstacles', discovering 'the only possible way of saying something as luminously as possible', expressing the 'small secrets' of childhood and the life-anchoring memories of erotic experience. Montague's poetry has been fit to take the strain of the big historical and political difficulties we have faced in common and to register with honesty and delicacy the most intimate felicities and desolations which we all know (and can only know) alone. The poems are a 'source, half-imagined and half-real', and what John once said in an early poem about his musician uncle can now be said about himself: he is one of those through whom 'succession passes'.

The Bag Apron or The Poet and His Community

As I began this lecture I became all too aware that there were few recent precedents for my present post. There were the lectures that became his book, *Literature in Ireland*, by the young poet-rebel Thomas MacDonagh, at University College Dublin; his successor, Austin Clarke, describes MacDonagh absentmindedly placing a revolver on the desk. Then there were the lectures given by Frank O'Connor as a guest of Trinity College, lectures gathered in *A Backward Look*, which are among the very best causeries on early Irish literature. But O'Connor was more a translator than a poet, and we want a forward not a backward look, especially at this time.

Later, I attended the extraordinary discourses of Patrick Kavanagh at UCD in the mid-fifties, performances organised by the then taoiseach, John A. Costello, because of his barrister's guilt at having grilled Kavanagh to nervous exhaustion during the poet's foolhardy libel action against an impoverished Dublin periodical. Patrick had lost a lung through cancer, and he coughed and spluttered like an ancient motorcar, or a thrashing machine, relaxing now and then to quaver a ballad in his broken voice. His audience was the wild young from the pubs ('Not to be exciting to the young is death', was his Blakean epigram), and they cheered their man on as the Irish writers of the day were toppled like ninepins. I will try not to follow his example, but it was an exhilarating performance, delivered with the unmistakable roar of that particular poetic animal. In other words, he sounded completely like himself.

This process of discovering your own voice is both psychic and physical. 'She speaks in her own voice / Even to strangers', says Robert

Graves of a friend, and that is the poet's task, to achieve authenticity, to speak in his own voice, 'the true voice of feeling', in his own rhythms. It is a primitive process, with many parallels in nature, like the reptile sloughing off scales, or the butterfly emerging from its chrysalis. For young poets are like all adolescents: they imitate their heroes, nearly becoming them. With what psychic greed and astonishment I fell upon James Joyce, whose Catholic upbringing in Clongowes seemed like my own in Armagh College. But imagine my disappointment when I learnt that the stews of Dublin had been cleaned up by the Legion of Mary, and that my own sexual education would be delayed. Meanwhile, Tom Kinsella thought he was Thomas Mann's Tonio Kröger, as he prowled around the streets of Inchicore.

These early imitative efforts, actually more like possession than imitation, slowly give way to the real thing; as if in a room crowded with ghosts, the poet begins to speak in his or her own voice. Milosz writes: 'all my life I have been in the power of a daimonion, and how the poems dictated by him came into being I do not quite understand.' The poet moves from being in thrall to the voices he or she admires, to possession by his or her own daimonion. My friend Gary Snyder speaks of how one discovers one's rattle or rhythm in a dream, the kind of power vision the American Indians describe. For your way of talking is allied to your way of walking, and is as basic as your breathing. And so, when they have come into their own, poets start to look like their poems, or the reverse.

This could be the basis of an intellectual parlour game. When I first heard the languid, sardonic, rasping voice of Louis MacNeice, forty-four years ago, I thought it sounded like the barking of a fox or a seal:

I am not yet born; O hear me.
Let not the bloodsucking bat or the rat or the stoat or the
    club-footed ghoul come near me.

['Prayer before Birth']

The gangly and cantankerous figure of Kavanagh, with his hunched shoulders, seemed as uncompromising as the abrasive rhythms of *The*

Great Hunger, just as the slow and melancholy movements of Austin Clarke were often echoed in his more private poems.

It could be amusing, but potentially dangerous, to move this intellectual parlour game to our own times. Ted Hughes looked and sounded like a Henry Moore rock sculpture from Yorkshire. Another American poet friend, the one-eyed Robert Creeley, is lean and over six foot two, and speaks hesitantly, as if he had marbles or precious stones in his mouth. I feel an affinity with him, because some of my more hesitating, wavering rhythms are linked to my stammer. Can one not say that the poems of Seamus Heaney often look as robust and sturdy as himself, as bulky as Robert Frost? Or that the verses of Michael Longley are as delicate yet ample as himself?

There are, of course, many obstacles to finding one's own voice, and they are partly due to education. The poets we responded to at school, where we had to endure poetry, had to have strong rhythms, like Alfred Noyes's 'The Highwayman':

The road was a ribbon of moonlight over the purple moor

Or:

His eyes were hollows of madness, his hair like mouldy hay,
But he loved the landlord's daughter,
    The landlord's red-lipped daughter

Or John Davidson's 'The Runnable Stag':

When pods went pop on the broom, green broom
    And apples began to be golden-skinned

Compressing my education through Garvaghey and Glencull Primary Schools to St Pat's Armagh, I think I had little or no sense of what poetry could mean, except as a hurdle in the exam stakes, or, occasionally, rhythms rousing as a song.

Indeed, you might say that we had a bias against poetry, and here I must introduce an important character in my development. Let us call him the Man from Keady, who voiced our disgust at having to deal with such rubbish; the Romantics especially were risible. His party piece was to recite Keats's 'Ode to a Nightingale' in a strong Ulster accent: 'Thou wast not born for death, immortal Bird! / No hungry generations tread thee down' he twanged.

As for Shelley's 'To a Skylark': 'Hail to thee, blithe Spirit,' he raised an imaginary shotgun, 'Bird thou never wert'. Phrases like 'charioted by Bacchus and his pards' (conjuring up some celestial gambling saloon) or 'Here where men sit and hear each other groan', scrawled on a lavatory wall, doubled us over with laughter.

Helen Vendler might not believe it, but I think that the Man from Keady was trying to make an important point through his parody: he was mocking a certain kind of English speech, was saying crudely that all this had nothing to do with him, that there was nothing in our English books which directly concerned us. But something in me seemed to stir when our Irish teacher, Sean O'Boyle, intoned the local South Armagh *aislingí* in class. I can still try to sing them, although they also seemed remote from our semi-urban, wartime existence, or any possible future. A few poems in the later part of our anthology, such as Stephen Spender's 'Landscape Near an Aerodrome' suggested a modern poetry, unlike the Chesterbelloc Catholic formula promulgated by our English master. (Many years later, sharing a platform with Sir Stephen, I thanked him so warmly that, in his turn at the podium, he praised the poems of 'John Montgomery'.)

You begin to find your own voice when you start to write not what you want to, but what you can, indeed must. In his Harvard lectures, Milosz speaks of 'the corner of Europe that shaped me and to which I have remained faithful by writing in the language of my childhood'. Or as Joyce said, in a famous exchange with a Waterford gentleman called Arthur Power who had come to Paris in order to learn how to write like Voltaire: 'You must write what is in your blood and not what is in your brain.'

[4]

For a gifted and insufferable youngster who read everything, this truth took a long time to understand. There were several stages in the unfurling of the layers of the self. As a happy little Ulster boy in wartime, I read everything I could find: I moved from cigarette cards of our fighting ships and planes, to Jules Verne and H. G. Wells, with their pseudo-scientific view of the world. After that I advanced to the middlebrow epics of A. J. Cronin; I saw *Dr Wassell* in the Ritz Cinema in Belfast.

But Master MacGurren had leaned over my shoulder in Glencull School to tell me about things called 'classics', implanting a deep curiosity. Soon the Tyrone Chief Librarian, a Mrs Tilly from Yorkshire, was wondering at the choice of books requested by my Aunt Winifred who ran our branch of the County Library. She could not believe that the local farmers were eager to plough through *War and Peace* and *Crime and Punishment* after a hard day in the fields.

It was still prose, of course, and the only part of Tolstoy's epic that I could relate to was Levin working in the harvest fields. The plot thickened when I moved to UCD and fell under the influence of my poetic contemporaries, and the spell of post-Emergency, melancholy Georgian Dublin, an atmosphere I try to convey in some of my earliest poems. But although Dublin was the first city I fell in love with, I was still eager for the larger world I had read and heard of, and to which I had briefly belonged, as a child in Brooklyn. I followed the tracks of the Sherman tanks, which had crushed our hedges in Tyrone, when I made my first journey by bicycle through the battlefields of northern France, in 1948, awed by the lines of white crosses and crumbling helmets that strangely resembled vineyards of various vintages, from 1870 to 1945.

Now I had decided that I was Rimbaud, but a Rimbaud who could hardly speak French. After working in the wine harvest or *vendanges* on the Marne, my companion and I descended in search of the fleshpots of Paris, hoping, maybe, for a black mistress, like Baudelaire's Jean Duval. Instead we were waylaid by a bisexual Dutch friend and brought to a gay nightclub called Dr Moons, where I had to defend the Armagh virginity I had hoped to lose. Coming back to London through Charing Cross, I stocked up on the grim deities of the time, Kafka and Rilke, and the first translations of Hölderlin by Michael Hamburger. What Myles called 'the gentle art of Kafkaing and Rilkeing' was necessary for survival in literary Dublin. Or as my friend Brendan Behan said of our generation: 'Only a few hours out of the bog, and they're up to their arses in angst.'

It was the beginning of the Third Programme, and, during my holidays, my long-suffering aunts endured those discords that often sounded through the farmhouse, replacing their own favourite programmes, such as *Question Time* and the *Mansion House Ceilidh*. And in Fintona, my father, home from America, built shelves to accommodate books like André Gide's *Journals*, that he did not dare open, for fear that they would offend his Catholic *pudeur*. I suppose the climax for me and many of my generation, like the painter Barrie Cooke, and Ted Hughes, was the publication in 1959 of ten Penguin editions of D. H. Lawrence. I began to see my own countryside through a sensual haze, to which, alas, the girls did not seem to respond. And when I showed *The Rainbow* to an older, farmer friend, Barney Horisk, he roundly declared, 'That man Lawrence knows buck-all about farming.'

Omnivorous, derivative, stumbling through French, German, Russian and Italian literature – to say nothing of the invading Americans – how did I extricate myself from this maelstrom of influences? It did not happen easily or quickly: precocity was nearly impossible during a period when so much was going on across the world. I admired the intense post-war literary life of France, startling in its energy, from Mauriac, Montherlant and Gide, to Sartre and Camus. Again mainly prose, but I carried away a key phrase: *Il faut cultiver vos obsessions*. In other words, you must write out of your own wellsprings, write about what you have to; and slowly but surely your subject matter emerges.

There was the landscape of my upbringing, the hills of Tyrone, or 'the wild west' as a Belfast man in the Crown Bar recently observed to me. A landscape with figures, of course, the branches of my broken family tree, a tree splintered by politics and history. And the old people who hobbled down to our post office, through whom I came to know an older Ireland, before it would be swept away by factory farming.

Sometimes that intense feeling for the Ulster and Irish landscapes trembles towards an ideal patriotism, what one calls *tír grá* in Irish, or love of the land. In this connection, I recall a fierce discussion I had with Ted Hughes in Listowel, County Kerry, before he accepted the laureateship. I maintained that no one could be a simple patriot anymore, and quoted his own poem, 'Out': 'Let England close. Let the green sea-anemone close.' He suggested that I was misreading the poem, which was really about the abomination of war, and began to speak of the British crown as a symbol of the unity of the tribe, like some ancient British chieftain: *Arturus, Dux Brittanniarum* … As if Ted Hughes was the Merlin of the lost kingdom of Elmet.

Simpler than *tír grá* was *grá* itself, the effort to love. While not subscribing to the muse theory of Robert Graves, even under tonight's full moon, one can still recognise that there is an affinity between love and the lyric, though that love need not be limited to the chivalrous impulse of courtly love. It can be domestic love, between husband and wife, it can be directed towards the old mine workings of W. H. Auden, the hovering falcon of Hopkins, or the battle-weary comrades of David Jones – even the Fintona Horse Tram – anyone or anything cargoed with feeling. Milton surprisingly declared that poetry should be 'simple, sensuous, and passionate', and it is this intensity that makes lines of Yeats ring in our ears, the most singable poet since the Elizabethans. Love of place, love of another – whether companion, child, or parent – love is the charge behind the lyric, technical mastery its muscle.

And there are deeper, underlying, almost inchoate concerns. Clio or History, for instance, is one of the Muses, but in this age of individual consciousness, public themes cannot be asserted, as in the *Aeneid*'s account of the founding of Rome, or the violent glory of war chronicled in the *Iliad*. My training as an historian in UCD helped, but I came to realise that for me as a poet history could only be 'his story', what I know about what had happened to my people, as I will explain later.

Then there are truly primitive and pre-historical powers working. Stones and water are among the enduring images in my work. Even when I translate, I instinctively turn to poems like the *Carnac* of Eugène

Guillevic, who was born beside those ancient stones. Guillevic was a socialist, but then all great socialist poets seem to write paeans of mystic materialism, like Hugh MacDiarmid's 'On a Raised Beach', Pablo Neruda's 'On the Heights of Macchu Picchu', or the long promontory of his Piedras Negras. And when I am drunk out of my mind, I see behind my closed eyes water flowing over stones, perhaps my version of Eden, my primal landscape.

And there is the central irony of my career: the effort to be fluent about speechlessness. Being here in Belfast has for me the haunting quality of the road not taken. Omagh and Armagh were my two towns, but in my last year at school, as the wars ended, I began to come regularly to Belfast for speech therapy. My therapist was a lively young woman who taught me breathing exercises, placing a professional but distracting hand on my diaphragm. She had a passion for both opera and war poetry, introducing me to *Penguin New Writing*, and poets like Drummond Allison and Alun Lewis. I still went to see her all through the summer, cycling to now-closed railway stations, such as Beragh and Sixmilecross, spending a crammed day in Belfast, often taking in a film, as well as the dirty pictures of the Smithfield Market.

I was becoming dimly aware of something called Ulster regionalism, but it seemed to deal mainly with matters east of the Bann, the Northern Pale, and was already fading. I called upon a gruff John Hewitt at the Ulster Museum, but he would soon go into exile, and it was in London or Dublin that I would meet MacNeice and Rodgers. So my poetic stirrings had to take place against the background of Dublin and UCD, where a new generation was beginning to emerge, not post-war, but a post-civil war that would take me years to understand. I did not know their provenance, but their passion for poetry was a prod in the right direction. Anthony Cronin from Enniscorthy spouting Auden, Ben Kiely singing MacNeice to MacNeice, John Jordan intoning Lorca, Pearse Hutchinson reciting everything! Despite the introverted gloom of post-Emergency Dublin, a new generation was cracking the egg, with the iconoclastic figure of Kavanagh as a goad. With such a cast of characters, my ambitions to be a bestselling novelist crumbled, although now I am glad to transfer them to my partner, Elizabeth.

My loneliness as a marooned northerner and apprentice southerner still kept me slightly apart. Gawky, red-haired, stammering in a Tyrone accent, I must have stood out amongst them: to the children of the new Free State, the North was a foreign country. And there was a further complication: my American birth. In due course, I would leave to explore that great country from end to end, meeting easier, less fractious contemporaries: Snodgrass and Bly in Iowa, Ginsberg and Snyder in San Francisco.

So you wander round the world to discover the self you were born with. But I had already made a start. I heard two of my poems being read out on Austin Clarke's poetry programme; another prize-winner was John Hewitt, which prompted my call on him in Belfast, when I was up to see my father in the Royal Victoria Hospital. And after my long American *hegira* I began again to publish poems, this time with an Ulster accent. Austin Clarke rang me up after he'd read 'The Sean Bhean Bhocht' in the *Irish Times*, a poem not about a national symbol, but a real poor old woman whom I had known:

As a child I was frightened by her
Busy with her bowl of tea in a farmhouse chimney corner,
Wrapped in a cocoon of rags and shawls.

I had travelled far in order to write about homely things.

One grew up slowly then, through a clamour of influences. My first wee book was called *Forms of Exile* (1958), something my generation specialised in, trying to escape the restrictions imposed by oppressive religio-political systems, both north and south, mirror-images of each other. But things were looking up. In 1960 a poem of mine won one of the first poetry prizes in this part of the world: the May Morton, and it was read by Sam MacCready in the Assembly Rooms of the Presbyterian Church in Belfast, though later it was docked a stanza in its transmission from the BBC North of Ireland. I was so pleased, I had it printed by my new pal, Liam Miller of the Dolmen Press, and sent one to Patrick Kavanagh. He stopped me in the street, to offer me a compliment: 'I see you got in the bag apron; I could never manage it meself.' Now that the bag apron had travelled all the way from Friel's Ballybeg to Broadway to Hollywood, it may seem a small matter, but it was a big step at the time.

Authenticity is the holy grail of the artist. To achieve 'Like Dolmens round my Childhood, the Old People', my experience of life in a country post office in County Tyrone and my dim sense of the deep archaeo-logical past of the Clogher Valley came together under the influence of poems as diverse as the early Anglo-Saxon, Alan Tate's *Ode to the Confederate Dead*, and the bruised gloom of Wilfred Owen's 'Strange Meeting'. There is a line in my early work through *Poisoned Lands* (1961), *Death of a Chieftain* (1964) to *The Rough Field* (1972), an explor-ation of the hidden Ulster west of the Bann, which, except for Ben Kiely, had not found expression since William Carleton's *Traits and Stories*.

In his study of the short story, *The Lonely Voice*, Frank O'Connor argues that the strength of the storyteller often comes from the pressure behind him of a community which has not achieved definition, a submerged population: Lawrence's coalminers, Joyce's mean Dubliners, Flannery O'Connor's Georgia grotesques. In the pre-literate Tyrone of my past, there was a primitive respect for the poet, a kind of laughter and fear aroused by the idea of the local bard. I had a cousin, Tommy Montague, who was known as the Bard of Altamuskin, and whose verses appeared in the *Ulster Herald*. He had harps inset on the walls of his house, and a glass-walled study where he wrote old-fashioned novels. People thought he was a bit cracked, but, God bless him, he lent me Lambs' *Tales from Shakespeare* while he wallpapered our parlour. Then there was Michael Mullen, the Bard of Foremass, and the Farrells of Glencull, one of whose songs is included in *The Rough Field*: 'Glencull Waterside'. There were also the slightly more sophisticated voices of Matt Mulcahy and Barney MacCool of Coolaghy in the *Tyrone Constitution*.

And of course the Reverend Marshall's excursions into the Ulster dialect haunt me still:

Consarnin' weemin, sure it wos
 A constant word of his,
'Keep far away from them that's thin,
 Their temper's aisy riz.'
[...]
An' Margit she wos very wee,
 An' Bridget she wos stout,
But [and here comes the epic smile] her face wos like a Jail dure
 With the bowlts pulled out.
['Me an' Me Da']

Both sides of the house had retained some dim respect for the idea of verse, if not poetry, and occasionally somebody would raise the old canard that we in mid-Ulster still spoke the language of Shakespeare. Didn't Marshall organise a reading from *A Midsummer Night's Dream*, with Matt Mulcahy, my old Fintona neighbour, as Bottom? (The satirical side of the bard would now be best expressed by comics, like the deadpan ironies of Kevin MacAleer.) The truth was that Tyrone had not known a professional poet since the days of the O'Neills, and through my long literary apprenticeship I was harnessing an artesian energy from many silent centuries. These hushed, orphaned voices whispered partly in another language, emphasising the ironies of my own name: Tadgh or Tague transformed into the more stylish Montague. The journey into this reservoir of silence was all the more ironical because I was born not in Ballygawley but Brooklyn, yet that distance may have made me listen more closely, like Sam Hanna Bell transported from Glasgow to the rural County Down of *December Bride*.

 Among the welter of the world's voices, in the streets, on the airwaves, in the press, you find your own voice, yet this does not isolate you, but restores you to your people. Across the world, the unit of the parish is being broken down by global forces, and from Inniskeen to Garvaghey, from Bellaghy to Ballydehob, to the Great Plains of America, an older lifestyle, based on the seasons, is being destroyed. But it can still be held in the heart and the head. Although I know I will never be able to satisfy the Man from Keady, I have (echoing Nennius, the early British historian, as quoted by David Jones) 'made a heap of all I could find', a cairn of the heart's affections.

A transcript of a lecture given in Queen's University, Belfast, on 5 November 1998.

Short Thoughts on the Long Poem
Words and Music

I SHORT THOUGHTS ON THE LONG POEM

I say 'short thoughts' because the subject is a book-length one, like C. M. Bowra's study of the epic, or Auerbach's *Mimesis*. All I can bring to it is my own experience thinking of, and trying to write, long poems – three in all so far, with one to come, perhaps.

The Greco-Roman or classical epic dominates our view of the long poem, beginning with Homer's *Iliad*, described by Simone Weil as a 'poem of force'. Then there is the *Odyssey*, a more psychological and personal epic, the influence of which persists to our own day, in Joyce's great *Ulysses*. And in the background there is always the presence of the other world, disputing gods and goddesses playing havoc with human beings, backing their favourites, an atmosphere found also in the great tragedies. Virgil's *Aeneid* descends from the same tradition, Aeneas being a character in the *Iliad*. It also celebrates force, the matter of Rome, beginning '*Arma virumque cano*', 'Arms and the man I sing', although the most moving scenes are of Dido's love, and the doomed Turnus. Again gods and goddesses capriciously intervene, as in some rigged gambling saloon: as Hopkins says, they are not gentle-folk, but 'unnatural rakes'! Then we have the three books of *La Divina Commedia*, although Hell and Purgatory are far from our sense of the comic. To indicate the continuity of the tradition, Virgil is Dante's guide through Hell and Purgatory, where Ulysses reappears and is given a different destiny. Again we have the presence of the otherworld, but now hardened into the mighty scholastic structure of medieval Catholicism, with its angels, saints and virgins.

The strength of such shared assumptions persisted until the middle of the twentieth century, or rather, could be said to haunt it, since the influence of Darwin, Frazier and Freud had made these beliefs so tenuous. Two poems by Americans who had emigrated to Europe evoke this broken tradition of the classical epic. Eliot's *The Waste Land* speaks of 'Falling towers / Jerusalem Athens Alexandria' but also reaches out towards meaning and salvation, which seem hard to find. *The Cantos of Ezra Pound*, a long 'poem including history', were begun in 1925, with a scene from the *Aeneid*, and evoking gods, goddesses, nymphs and sages from many societies, a poetic equivalent of Malraux's *Museum without Walls*. But all his luminaries and talismanic figures, like Kung and Jefferson, and the Adams family, cannot be made to add up to a vision of order in our age: 'I cannot make it cohere', is Pound's terrible cry in the late *Cantos*. The collapse of a whole system, Greco-Roman in structure, and Judeo-Christian in belief, haunts these poems. The so-called Modern Movement of the early twentieth century is as neo-classical as the Augustan age, with its rage for order (Wallace Stevens before Derek Mahon) and its revival of imitation as a technique.

The desire for an English epic, encompassing and celebrating the matter of Britain, is something that recurs throughout English poetry. *Beowulf* belongs in the context of saga, or the home-made folk epic. The central English myth is Arthurian, whether you follow Geoffrey of Monmouth, or Malory who inspired Tennyson. I must make a confession here: when I was reading E. M. Tillyard on Milton, I was fascinated by those pages where he shows the great poet trying to find his theme, being long-tempted by the Arthurian before settling on his great Protestant subject. (Like Dante, he fell back on the Bible, though, unlike that angry Florentine, he did not commit his own contemporaries to hell or purgatory.) I would like to think that as a little Ulster boy I became infected with Puritanism, and like Seamus Deane I can still read *Paradise Lost* in Protestant Ulster. Milton's is the most deliberately epic effort in English, invoking the example of the ancients in his preface: 'The measure is English heroic verse without rhyme, as that of Homer in Greek, and of Virgil in Latin.' Milton has '*la longue haleine*', the long breath of the epic.

The Arthurian cycle still persists in the work of David Jones's *Sleeping Lord*, and in English, Welsh, Cornish and Breton mythology. But why is there no great long poem about Arthur which is the English equivalent of the *Iliad*? One would have to conclude that while there are many fine long English poems, especially Romantic ones such as the *Prelude* and *Don Juan*, there does not seem to be an English national epic, encompassing that country's myths and history. I have described how Milton hesitated over the Arthurian theme, but instead chose the Fall of Man: *Paradise Lost* could be regarded as the English Protestant epic. (And it is of course composed in iambic verse, which, though a heavier style than Shakespeare's, makes sonorous public reading, especially when Satan speaks, and the love scene in Paradise.)

There are other, less daunting long poems in English. Chaucer learnt from Ovid and Boccaccio how to weave tales together, and Langland has his wonderful medieval vision, a major influence on David Jones. But *The Faerie Queene*, meant to be the great English renaissance poem, is even more daunting than Milton. Although I have lived beside the Lee, and seen Spenser's home in North Cork, I still prefer his shorter poems to his intended masterpiece. He wanted to write a Romantic epic, like Ariosto and Tasso, but he lacked the lightness of movement, and chose a lovely but slow-moving stanza, which was bound to obstruct his narrative, while the argument or structure he proposed was too weighty for any tale.

Every country, every nation, perhaps every province, aspires to an epic. Similar desires arise in music, with Sibelius echoing the *Kalevala*, Lönnrot's gathering of the tales of Finland. The northern folktales of the *Nibelungenlied* resonate throughout Wagner. But back to poetry. In Poland there is the *Pan Tadeusz* of Mickiewicz, with its epic bear hunt translated by Donald Davie. From hunting to seafaring, the imperial voyages of Portugal are celebrated in the *Lusiad*, a direct echo of the *Aeneid*. But perhaps the most persuasive of all is the *Mahabharata*, the great Vedic or Indian tale, which is also a religious statement, puppet-versions of which can be bought at street stalls. There, there are enough triple gods and goddesses, cowherds and *gopis*, to make even the deities of Olympus blush, rituals that attracted a director like Peter Brook.

Many of these peripheral sagas or home-grown epics are concerned, like the *Iliad* or the *Aeneid*, with the clash of war. France has very few longer poems, but the best is the *Chanson de Roland*, dealing with the eternal strife between the Moorish and Gallic worlds. As for the matter of Ireland, one of the great achievements of modern Irish literature is Kinsella's translation of the *Táin*, which illustrates the Irish theory of the epic, or long poem, using prose until the chariot wheels catch fire. If Spenser had learnt more Irish, he might have lit a fire under the Faerie Queene's tale.

The modern long poem is mainly American, the *Cantos* of Pound, the *Paterson* of his friend, William Carlos Williams, *The Maximus Poems* of Charles Olson. These are all poems about history, or at least a definition of a culture, and they all wage an only partly successful war against the iambic line, which, according to Williams, was not the natural tempo of American speech. There were false starts, such as Longfellow's *Hiawatha*, but the most original of contemporary long poets, perhaps the father of all modern epic poetry, was Walt Whitman, with his *Leaves of Grass*, a pantheistic and democratic vision of the universe. We know he loved the rhythmical structures of the Old Testament, and he adored opera, which may have inspired his exuberant arias, like 'Song of Myself'. 'He had his nerve,' says Randall Jarrell, but he succeeded in doing what neither Pound nor MacDiarmid would manage, to weave a long poem out of the strands of himself. Although it contains beautiful individual volumes, like 'Drum Taps' from the Civil War, *Leaves of Grass* does add up, ironically as unified as the work of that decadent dandy in Paris, Baudelaire, with his *Fleurs du Mal* – flowers of evil instead of leaves of grass.

America, being seemingly the most modern country, was fascinated by the adventure of modern poetry, and the most influential long poem of recent Anglo-American literature is, of course, T. S. Eliot's *The Waste Land*, which was originally called (before Pound's surgical editing) *He Do the Policeman in Many Voices*. Eliot was part of a great generation: Pound, Stevens, Williams, Hart Crane. These last two especially thought that, when all the bets were off, Eliot had handed back modern poetry to the academy. They thought of him as a traitor to the tenets of modernism. Crane's hymn to *The Bridge*, under whose shadow I was born, is an attempt to find a myth to replace the classical. In his letters you can follow his agonised debate with the implications of *The Waste Land*. And in *Paterson*, Williams tries to show that no land is waste; even in the most featureless American town, emotion blooms.

There is a line running through contemporary American poetry, from the optimistic vision of *Leaves of Grass*, through *Paterson*, to the desolation of Ginsberg's *Fall of America*. In my Californian days, my pals were people like Ginsberg and Snyder and Robert Duncan, all of whom seemed to be writing long poems. Olson's theory of open form – it seemed to me a contradiction in terms – was much debated, although I thought his better work was the earlier, more compact poems, like 'Kingfishers'. They were a fine company of poets, but I was not sure about their practice. Snyder was working on a long poem called *Mountains and Rivers without End*, based upon the idea of unfurling a Chinese scroll. 'At least mine will be ended before yours,' I said prophetically.

Then there is the Irish long poem. I spoke of the *Táin*, and there was a time when I hoped to weave together an even greater bundle of stories, the Fenian tales, especially the 'Conversation between the Old Men', Oisín and Patrick, which Máirtín Ó Cadhain thought was the greatest work in Irish. And there are lesser stories, like the 'Frenzy of Sweeny', and the 'Vision of Mac Conglinne'. There is even an Irish version of the *Aeneid*.

In the eighteenth century, the two traditions and languages co-existed: the Anglo-Irish lament, *The Deserted Village*, the fierce pre-feminist humour of *The Midnight Court*, the heart-scalding drum beat of the 'Lament for Art O'Leary'. Allingham's *Laurence Bloomfield* has the amplitude of a Victorian novel. But when Patrick Kavanagh comes to write *The Great Hunger*, he channels both the erotic and economic frustrations of life on a small farm. I can testify from seeing the American anthologies in his flat that he was addicted to modern American poetry, and had read *The Waste Land*. Remember the scene in *The Green Fool*, when he asks for *The Waste Land* in the National Library?

'Without invention, nothing is well spaced.' Technical solutions are largely dictated by the material. Much as I loved Hart Crane, I could not be dithyrambic about Garvaghey, County Tyrone. Under my eyes it was becoming a no-place, like Paterson, or as Gertrude Stein said of Oakland, 'there's no there, there'. And there was not the belief that would underpin earlier long poems of the Christian period, but a conflict of attitudes, which I illustrate in 'The Bread God'.

II WORDS AND MUSIC

Poetry flourishes where there is a natural connection between poetry and speech, the rhythms of the human voice, as in the Elizabethan period, when ordinary speech seemed to flow or fall naturally into iambics so that ostensibly abstract language could be understood even by the groundlings. The poetry that Shakespeare published in his own lifetime is much less accessible to the reader than the plays assembled by others in the First Folio, perhaps because the poet was being more self-consciously literary when he composed his arcane verses, like *The Phoenix and the Turtle*, whereas the plays were invigorated by profes-sional need, the pressure of many voices.

There is also another consideration, the relationship between poetry and music, which, practically speaking, assists the fluency of the verse. Behind much of Elizabethan poetry, one hears the phantom plucking of a lute or a psaltery, while many poems in Irish, especially in the seventeenth and eighteenth centuries, were also songs. Thomas MacDonagh, the most gifted of the poet martyrs of Easter 1916, has written on the connection between poetry and music in his *Literature in Ireland*; as well as Irish poetry, in both languages, he had studied the Elizabethan lyricist Campion. A change came when Cromwell and his pleasure-loathing ilk closed the theatres, and poetry returned to the intimacy of manuscript. Playwriting had been a public act, and publication in our modern sense of the book was still embryonic; besides, publication could be considered *infra dig* for a courtier. So Donne's poems were circulated, as were Marvell's. The critical unease of Ben Jonson, even with Shakespeare, is based on his being one of England's first professional poets, earning his living as such.

Poetry always has a political aspect. As the Scottish poet Hugh MacDiarmid has said, 'Any utterance that is not propaganda is impure propaganda for sure.' The political aspect was so prominent in the eighteenth century that many of the more successful poems of the period have the effect of pamphlets. The heroic couplet, introduced under the French influence of Charles II's court, gave a crispness to the message of poems such as Dryden's *Absalom and Achitophel* and Pope's *The Rape of the Lock*. But the restraining influence of the rhyming couplet, which has come to seem a necessity for poetry in the popular mind, is not entirely natural to English verse, and perhaps the greatest lyric poetry occurs where the naturalness of speech is only partly corseted by form, as in the best of Yeats.

The Romantic poets did not presume an audience, although Byron had one, being as potent an image in his day as Mick Jagger. Those we call the Lake Poets seemed to prefer isolation, especially Wordsworth, who often composed out of doors, as he strode along; a neighbour describes him as 'booming like a bee'. This brings us to the crucial question of the poet's voice, which is determined by his own bodily and psychic rhythms, the cadences of his heart and head. (There is a sense in which the poems should look like the person who composed them. The long lines of the American poet Robert Creeley, like a Giacometti figure, resemble his own lean form, while the short, gnomic verses of Guillevic echo the poet's short, taut steps.)

The first recording we have of a poet in English is Tennyson reading that very jingoistic poem, *The Charge of the Light Brigade*. His strong Lincolnshire accent and rhythms stayed with him all his life, as did Yeats's strong, slow-cadenced Sligo accent in the fragments that have survived from the programmes he recorded for the BBC. Since then,

there have been many recordings of poets, especially those done by our own Claddagh Records in Dublin, on the principle that the poet should be heard reading his own work in his own voice, with its own rhythms.

In dramatising *The Rough Field*, I tried to do the same, blending or at least contrasting various voices. Like the harsh rasp of Pat Magee for whom Beckett wrote *Krapp's Last Tape*, the storytelling charm of Ben Kiely with his honeyed singing voice, the young Seamus Heaney from Derry, and of course my own Tyrone-bred self. And weaving through all that matter of Ulster, the tunes played by the Chieftains. In other words, I was trying to compose and record an *Ulsteriad*, using a variety of forms and voices to suggest the complexity of the history of Ulster, thus placing the poem in the western tradition of epic. For the problems raised by the matter of Ulster are many: Celt and Saxon, English and Irish, Catholic and Protestant, the clash of the female and male principles inherent in these religions. The pressure of a community is often in inverse proportion to its size, and if anyone doubts the complexity of the struggle in Ulster, on Europe's western edge, they have only to drive through the small towns and villages of the North. The Catholic ghettos flaunt the colours of Palestine, while the Bible-thumping loyalist enclaves are emblazoned with Israel's Star of David. Perhaps you could argue that this is history repeating itself as comedy, after tragedy, but the shafts that the Ulster problems send into the history of Western Europe are deep, and still unresolved, except in the harmonies of poetry and music.

A transcript of a lecture given in University College Dublin on 22 February 2001.

The Challenge of Translation

I have been involved in and engaged with translation for all of my creative life. The process has been a respite, a rest from my own work, but more often a challenge: how could this or that poem be made over into English? The great fertility of the Elizabethan period seems to me to come partly from that flow of other languages, Latin, French, Italian, into English. And when it comes to the Romantics, it is also the German language, Coleridge of course, and even Wordsworth composing the most exciting passage of *The Prelude* in Goslar. (Sometimes being surrounded by another language sharpens and strengthens one's sense of one's own. Think of Byron and Shelley in Italy, Joyce and Beckett in France.)

The obvious challenge for an Irish poet is the older language in which most of our earlier poetry was composed: our tradition is double-barrelled, or hybrid. I remember the Armagh afternoon when our Irish teacher, Sean O'Boyle, began to sing in class, chanting harshly beautiful songs that were actually poems from South Armagh. That region is now known to the outside world as 'bandit country' but it was originally the site or seat of a Court of Poetry, to which Creggan Churchyard still bears witness.

These were very formal poems, a bit like the contemporaneous verses of eighteenth-century England, Gray's *The Bard* or the more Scottish poems of James Thomson. But I was totally bowled over by the 'Lament for Art O'Leary', a wake song for a murdered man. Not until I read Lorca's dirge for his bullfighter friend would I meet its equal. Peter Levi declared 'Caoineadh Airt Uí Laoghaire' one of the great poems of the world. I felt I had to hammer out my own version, though always halting even over the very first line. Should '*Mo ghrá go daingean tu!*' be 'My steadfast love'; 'My stalwart love'; 'My love, my stronghold' or; 'My dauntless love'? That phrase echoes throughout the poem, as in the passage describing how the speaker finds her dead husband, the cry of a woman whose heart has been seared:

> My steadfast friend!
> I never believed you dead
> Until your horse came towards me,
> Trailing its bridle;
> Your heart's blood splashed
> From bit to polished saddle
> In which you rose and fell:
> I gave a leap to the threshold,
> A second to the gate,
> A third upon the horse.

Early Irish poetry came later. When I undertook *The Faber Book of Irish Verse* I decided to overhaul the whole of Irish poetry although, lacking the exhaustive scholarship necessary for such a task, I obviously could not always succeed. Kinsella was working on the *Táin* at the same time, and I felt honoured to be involved in a somewhat similar enterprise, spiriting the power of our past literature over into the present. And of course Irish is the oldest vernacular in the west, and I loved the pen-point accuracy of the earliest lyrics, their precision and delicacy:

> In Loch Leane
> a queen went swimming;
> a redgold salmon
> flowed into her
> at full of evening.
> (from the *Félire Aengus*)

[John Montague, 'Sunset']

Translating from the French was based upon a different impulse. Dazzled and dazed by the achievement of Joyce and the not yet acclaimed Beckett, I found my way to France after the Second World War. I had had only a few classes in French during my last year at school, but I was fascinated by the drama of nineteenth-century French poetry, which seemed more glamorous to an eager adolescent than the poets of Victorian England. After *vendanges* along the Marne, harvesting the pale grapes for champagne, I descended on Paris on my bicycle, like Rimbaud swooping down from Charleville. I had his complete works in my rucksack, with a daft introduction by Paul Claudel claiming that Rimbaud was an embryonic mystic. I had begun to read Baudelaire's condemned poems as well, perhaps hoping that I, too, would find an exotic mistress, and I also sported the black flag of Nerval's melancholy. As I have said, both Baudelaire and Nerval seemed much more exciting than their English counterparts; the former drinking absinthe or black coffee and either working all night or making love to his sultry mistress, the latter sauntering through Paris with his lobster on a lead before hanging himself from a lamp post!

I did not really try to translate *les poètes maudits*, these 'blighted bards', since many better hands had been there before me. But I became conscious that when the Modern Movement was beginning, France was a major influence: Flaubert on Joyce, Laforgue on Eliot, Gautier on Pound, and so on. Then quite suddenly there was a halt in the dialogue, and even a growing distrust. For instance, when I broached to Charles Monteith (the famous editor who fostered Golding and Heaney) a proposal for a *Faber Book of French Verse* to follow the success of my Irish one, his off-the-cuff dismissal was memorably succinct: 'I am afraid French poetry does not go down well in England. It would sell even less than Welsh.' And when, at his request, I sent a shoal of poems by my French poet pals to Alan Ross at the *London Magazine*, he commented dryly: 'The French really have peculiar poets.'

The initial problem is that the French expect the poet to be supremely intelligent. The marmoreal perfection of Mallarmé is an obvious example, but there is also Valéry's cry for clarity in his 'Complete Poem':

The sky is bare. The smoke floats. The wall shines.
Oh! How I should like to think clearly!

This attitude leads to the complexity of 'Le Cimetière Marin' or 'Seaside
Cemetery' as Mahon calls it, with its motto from Pindar, and invocation
of Zeno, the pre-Socratic philosopher. Rising at dawn to examine your
own mind is a strenuous idea of the poetic vocation. And how far this is
from Keats, who longs for a life of 'sensations' rather than of 'thoughts'.
It seems that the Anglophone poet aspires to pure feeling, whereas the
French poet desires pure thought, from Mallarmé and Valéry, to present
mandarins like Jacques Roubaud and Michel Deguy.

I should reveal a prejudice. It seems to me that the great generation
of French poets born on the hinge of the twentieth century, from
writers like Jouve, Éluard, Aragon, Michaux, Ponge, to Follain, Char
and Guillevic, are much more powerful than their contemporaries in
English, aspiring to Plato's ideal of the Philosopher Kings. (It is in this
company that Beckett found a natural place, translating Éluard and
producing a belated prose poem of his own, *A Fizzle*, in which he
declares morosely, 'I gave up before birth.') Surely they deserve a major
bilingual anthology of their own? Stephen Romer, an English poet who
teaches at Tours, has made a handsome start with his Faber anthology,
and I have done my bit as well, contributing to the two translation
series, Wake Forest in America and Bloodaxe in England, which have
been trying to cross the divide.

For instance, there is the fascinating problem of the prose poem, a
form beloved of the French since Baudelaire, but seldom found in
English. It gave me great pleasure to translate some of Ponge's most
endearing *pièces*, like 'The Horse', where that sly old Huguenot compares
the Pope on his throne to an equine posterior, or in other words, a
horse's ass. And his marvellous meditation on 'The Nuptial Habits of
Dogs' makes me cry with laughter. Those translations, together with C.
K. Williams's versions of *Le Parti Pris de Choses*, are reprinted in a Faber
paperback, which seems, alas, to have received very little notice in England.

And then of course there is Eugène Guillevic's *Carnac*, that gnomic masterpiece by someone who was brought up amongst those mysterious standing stones, which I translated for the Bloodaxe series. I have also done his *Les Murs*, or *The Walls*, for a recent exhibition of Dubuffet. The erotic complexity of Jouve, the Norman terseness of Follain, the Burgundian gloom of Frénaud, I have tried from time to time to translate or transfer their qualities into English, and will continue to do so, as well as translating my near contemporaries, like Michel Deguy, Robert Marteau, and Claude Esteban. In one of Claude's last sequences, *Sur La Dernière Lande*, he seems to have combined sensation and thought. Although written in the lamenting voice of King Lear, it finishes with hope:

And maybe all was written in the book
but the book was lost

or someone threw it in the brambles
without reading it

no matter, that which was written
abides, even

hidden, another who has not lived
through all that

and without knowing the book's language, will understand
each word

and when he has read it, something
of ours will yield

a breath, a kind of smile between the stones.
                    ['And Maybe All Was Written']

This optimistic note is not heard so much in the early Esteban. His first book, *La Saison Dévastée* or *The Stricken Season*, is very much the work of an alienated French intellectual:

> Tree, bird, field:
> There is only this boat
> Mounting the black current.
>
> Disjointed head, you
> Have come far –
>
> ['The Horizontal Sky']

In his later years he suffered a terrible loss, the violent death of his wife, commemorated in *Elégie de la Mort Violente*. Yet despite this almost annihilating pain, he achieves a note of whimsical sadness, which prepares the way for his King Lear sequence:

> When one has suffered too long, one should
> pause sometimes, and laugh a little, and share
> with friends some sweet cake since one is drinking
> sweet wine from the Canaries and let there be dances
> even a shade wanton, so once spoke a fool
> to distract his master who did not mend
> or who did not wish to mend from his malady,
> I know others like that.
>
> ['Someone Begins to Speak in a Room']

Michel Deguy is editor of the longest-lived poetry magazine in France, called simply *Poésie*, the only simple thing about Deguy's approach to poetry. His 'Royal Song', for example, begins by invoking many precedents:

> The poet in profile
> Set square to the body and the shadow on the sill

The poet Gulliver retracing the pattern of winter brambles
        with the pencil tip of Hopkins
Or shrinking to align the grass and the Zodiac
        with the compasses of Gongora
A genie of Persian tales rejecting indifference

A *philosophe* by training, Michel does not shirk the responsibility of our
intellectual heritage, and describes poetry, or the act of writing, as
follows:

The belief is that this mental swarm, this ball of soot and fire, this
obscurity that passes through the brain for an instant – *uno intuitu* –
then the long labour of unravelling, of description, a devious and
detailed analysis, ready to act again, with retro-active force, will
bring to a close the decoding, the post *partitum*, to only make an
intelligible mouthful.

Yet despite this intellectual intensity, Deguy, like Esteban, was harrowed
by the untimely death of his wife, which resulted in a departure from
his previous work, a remarkable series of anguished prose poems, that
form which seems to come naturally to the French poetic imagination.
    Then there is Robert Marteau, from the Charente, who shares many
of the mystical, even alchemical, ideas of Yeats, connecting them to the
mysteries of earth, as in his native place, the forest of Chize. He is also
profoundly influenced by ritual, an aficionado of the bullfight. Solitary,
indeed almost hermetical, Robert is as intense in his way as Deguy, deeply
conscious of how much we have lost in our exploitation of the world:

I say: nothing is tragic
Since man's skull lost
        the shape of the sky
I say
and (you will curse me)
Eve's blessing on the treasure

I say to the angel
you are Thoth, you are great Hermes
whom the serpents obey – and this quill.

['Memorial']

I continue to translate from the Irish, of course; there is a com-
radely exchange between Irish poets in the two languages. Nuala Ní
Dhomhnaill, for instance, my successor in this Chair, has been trans-
lated by the top brass of Irish poetry in English. My own efforts include
'The Broken Doll' and her lovely love poem, 'Blodewedd' (the Welsh
Lady of Flowers). Trying to describe how Blodewedd exfoliates in her
ardour, I borrowed a line from the American poet James Wright:

At the least touch of your fingertips
I break into blossom,
my whole chemical composition
transformed.
I sprawl like a grassy meadow
fragrant in the sun;
at the brush of your palm, all my herbs
and spices spill open

I read this aloud sometimes, startling my audience with a seeming sex
change, since the final stanza opens with:

Hours later I linger
in the ladies toilet,
a sweet scent wafting
from all my pores

And this ambiguity in translation recalls me to my own 'The Trout', in
which the speaker grasps the fish with his bare hands. Readers of the
poem in English have wondered if it is a thinly veiled description of
masturbation, but in the French of La Pléiade it is called 'La Truite',

meaning that that particular argument does not arise. I find Cathal Ó Searcaigh interesting because he writes in Ulster Irish, the Irish I tried to learn as a boy. In translating his 'Clabber: The Poet at Three Years', with its echo of Rimbaud's 'Les Poètes de Sept Ans', I tried, of course, to render it in my own English Ulster-Speak:

> ... I heard a squelch in my wellies
> and felt through every fibre of my duds
> the cold tremors of awakening knowledge.
>
> O elected clabber, you chilled me to the bone.

I also contributed to Michael Davitt's *Selected Poems* and, sad to say, helped to translate his last sequence of poems, about his wanderings in Gascony. Perhaps it is fitting to end with these lines, the acute observations of an Irishman abroad in France:

> Below us in the street
> the argot of the teenagers,
> bee swarm of their scooters
>
> up and down.
> In the morning three old soldiers,
> returning from the *Boulangerie*
>
> with their rifles of bread,
> stand to attention beneath our window,
> intently talking.

['Seimeing Soir']

A lecture written for The Poet's Chair.

Samuel Beckett, Neighbour

Hugh Kenner has a book on T. S. Eliot, the invisible poet. For us, growing up in the forties and early fifties in Ireland, Samuel Beckett was the Invisible Writer, the Greta Garbo of modern literature. None of his work was in print. There was a grim story going the rounds that he had been stabbed in Paris, and a party given in the Bailey by Oliver St John Gogarty to celebrate his possible demise. Austin Clarke told me that he had nearly taken a libel action against Beckett's English publisher because of the cruel portrait of him as Austin Ticklepenny, the Pot Poet of Dublin, in the novel *Murphy*, and Austin still referred to him as Sam Bucket. Then, at a Dublin party, I met Con Leventhal and his wife, Ethna McCarthy, both of whom I already knew as contributors to the *Dublin Magazine*, where some of my own early poems had appeared. They both spoke warmly of their great friend and contemporary at Trinity, and encouraged me to look him up in Paris on an obscure street, something like 'Favourite'? For I was planning my attack on post-war France, with a rucksack and a new racing bicycle I had bought with the proceeds of an English literature prize.

Although banned in Ireland, copies of *Murphy* were being passed from hand to hand. I found one myself in the stalls of Charing Cross, only to have it snaffled by a brother poet, who later kept my first edition of *Under the Volcano*, so he had good taste. I also found a copy of Beckett's youthful essay on Proust, a lovely little book with a dolphin on the cover. But my real triumph was to arrange to have myself locked in the back room of the National Library, where all the banned books were racked like slumbering bombs. 'The fiercest literary censorship this side of the Iron Curtain – and I do not exclude Spain,' wrote Robert Graves from Majorca in a letter to the *Irish Times* in 1950.

I would take this strange scene as a symbol of the intellectual isolation of our new neo-Catholic state, which had helped to drive Beckett out of Ireland. In search of a prose *persona*, I hovered between the scholastic arrogance of Stephen Dedalus and Belacqua, the prone polyglot protagonist of *More Pricks Than Kicks*. I have since re-found the cryptic epigrams I culled during that curious isolation, like 'Any fool can turn the blind eye, but who knows what the ostrich sees in the sand?' and they can still turn my head.

When I began to explore France in 1948 and later in 1950 during the so-called Holy Year, I enquired about Beckett, but there was little to learn. Con Leventhal said that Beckett had brought a new novel out of the war, but I could not track him down, as I did Francis and Madeleine Stuart, in their *chambre de bonne*, near the École Militaire. I read Francis a self-absorbed new poem of my own on suffering and starvation – 'In learning hunger one learns other things' – while their Siamese cats mated noisily in the background. But extracts from *Watt* were appearing in the little magazines of the post-war period, like John Ryan's *Envoy* in Dublin, and *Merlin* in Paris. There was a small group around that review: Patrick Bowles (who later was to help to translate *Molloy* into English), Austryn Wainhouse, Richard Seaver, a lean Scot called Alex Trocchi, all of whom spoke of Beckett, and some of whom had glimpsed, or even met him, with his polo neck and prison haircut. And of course Sinbad Vail, the son of Peggy Guggenheim, had also heard of him, although Beckett did not appear in his little yellow-covered review, *Points*, where early Behan erotica had been published. I did find two copies of Georges Duthuit's post-war *Transition* with his extraordinary *Three Dialogues* on art with Beckett, where the Frenchman serves as a stooge for Beckett's uncompromising views, startling to a starter like myself, but echoing some of the more intransigent theorems in his Proust essay. (One of the copies contains a bleak prose monologue by Suzanne Dumesnil, Beckett's future wife, which sounds like his later self; clearly they thought alike.)

As my Dublin pals poured into Saint-Germain that summer of 1950, they met, and occasionally mated, with the French lot and the new wave of American ex-pats. Daniel Mauroc, the poet of the *quartier*, strode by in his black cloak. We heard about Richard Wright, we saw James Baldwin, but there was nary a sign of Beckett, and of course I had lost his address. Already the myth of the aloof hermit was growing, and there was a rumour that he was writing in French, having given up English in disgust. I would not be around when the shock of *Godot* began to reverberate in the salons: I had fled as far away as San Francisco.

IN THE WINGS

Little did I know that, a decade later, this mysterious recluse would be my neighbour: I define 'neighbour' as someone living nearby or nigh. After the move to our rue Daguerre studio in 1961, I began to recognise my artistic neighbours. There was Eugène Guillevic, the poet from Brittany, plump as a bullfrog but walking with delicate steps; lean Bill Hayter, the engraver, an old Cornish hand; Brassaï, writer, artist, photographer of the old night life and walls of Paris; smiling Ionesco with his Asian wife; Simone de Beauvoir in her sober garb, like a lay sister. Such a concentration of genius in a small area was characteristic of Montparnasse; Picasso, Mondrian, Grosz and Chirico had all lived in the *quartier* a few decades before.

It was against this background that I finally glimpsed Beckett. Passing the American bar of the Dôme, I came to a halt as I saw two heads bent together in close colloquy, Beckett and Giacometti, who also lived nearby, with his brother Diego. I knew they liked each other, but to see them huddled together so intently was awesome, Beckett's stripped profile and Alberto's corrugated countenance. Were they discussing the tree in the Odéon production of *Godot*, or the racing results of the PMU?

I also became conscious that Beckett, like myself, was a great walker. I would see him here or there walking through the city, often far from our home base. One day I glimpsed him by the children's pool in the Luxembourg Gardens, standing still as a heron, watching the toy boats. The conventions of our village, our *quartier*, which I was beginning to understand, demanded discretion, so I passed by, but was moved enough to write a sonnet, 'Salute, in Passing, for Sam', which is almost transparent in meaning compared with Beckett's own more oblique and learned poems.

> The voyagers we cannot follow
> Are the most haunting. That face
> Time has worn to a fastidious mask
> Chides me, as one strict master
> Steps through the Luxembourg.
> Surrounded by children, lovers,
> His thoughts are rigorous as trees
> Reduced by winter. While the water
> Parts for tiny white-rigged yachts
> He plots an icy human mathematics –
> Proving what content sighs when all
> Is lost, what wit flares from nothingness:
> His handsome hawk head is sacrificial
> As he weathers to how man is.

At that time I was editing that anthology of the *nouvelle vague* of Irish writing, and I dropped off the bold, red-covered *Dolmen Miscellany* at 38, Boulevard St Jacques, just round the corner, and a correspondence began. Beckett's epistolary style was to the point. He liked the anthology, approved of its aims, and my own essay on Goldsmith had given him 'great pleasure'. Heady stuff for a younger writer to hear, so I took my heart in my hands and sent him the Luxembourg Gardens poem. He liked that too, and soon we were arranging to meet, now and again, on neutral ground for a chat. Everything connected with those early meetings was punctilious and formal. I called him between twelve and one, and he suggested a meeting place, usually nearby, the Closerie des

Lilas, a well-appointed temple to literature with its commemorative plaques everywhere, or the side bar of La Coupole.

I remember very little of what we said, except our seemingly mutual embarrassment. Mr Beckett was painfully shy, shy as an adolescent, twitching, touching things, rearranging objects on the table, a nervous habit of my own, so that it began to look like a game of phantom chess. In his essay on Proust, which had just been reprinted, and which I had reviewed in *The Guardian*, he seemed to argue that conversation was impossible, with an always changing subject confronting an eternally shifting object. And since I was not involved in the theatre, I had little or no Green Room gossip. Besides, I stammered, so we found ourselves in the absurd situation of someone who found it hard to speak engaging someone who did not believe in conversation, and certainly not in small talk. Sometimes there were long silences between us, as though we were gazing together down some deep well.

But though I felt vaguely uneasy about these silences, we gradually found common ground. We discussed Synge, whom he described as 'a nice man', like Goldsmith; he was especially fond of his prose writings on Wicklow, and spoke warmly of some of the lesser-known plays, like *The Well of the Saints*. I began to realise that Beckett's late and unexpected success as a dramatist was based on his student years in Dublin. He described how he would slip away to attend first nights in the Abbey, including several of the Yeats plays, and the controversial early performance of *The Plough and the Stars* in 1926, when he was only nineteen. The old Abbey seemed to him an almost holy place, and he was shocked when I gave him my opinion that the fire in the Green Room had not been extensive, but had been used as a ploy to build a new theatre, which should not have required the destruction of the old. I told him how I had raced down from my digs on that fateful morning to inspect the damage, but did not mention that I had met Austin Clarke on the same mission. He was also fascinated to hear that I had been at the funeral of his dear friend, the painter Jack B. Yeats, in Herbert Street. But I did not mention that the boisterous Behan, seeing the solemn assembly in their mourning clothes outside the Peppercanister church, had saluted them cheekily, with a query of 'head or harp?' as if they were street urchins playing pitch and toss.

Beckett was now deeply involved in the translations of his own works, an annoying but necessary procedure for someone of his exactitude. The South African writer Patrick Bowles had worked with him on *Molloy*, but found it daunting. Patrick said that Beckett would not accept any compromise in his relentless search for the right word. Especially hard were the jokes, which were scattered like raisins throughout the text. With his extraordinary command of both languages, Beckett couldn't rest until he had found an equivalent in the other tongue: he lived balanced between French and English, a bilingual bicycle. Because of his lengthy exile, he now spoke a pure Hiberno-English of a certain vintage, free of more recent slang, whereas his French, through his wartime need to survive, had grown less academic and more colloquial.

Beckett also encouraged me to contact Maurice Nadeau at *Les Lettres Nouvelles*, and would later recommend my poems to Jerome Lindon of Les Éditions de Minuit. Altogether, it was the strained, serious conversation of *deux hommes des lettres*. And although we had two or three drinks, we remained careful and decorous in our exchanges.

THE IRISH WEREWOLF

The advent of Con Leventhal changed all that. The abbreviation of Cornelius to Con was a legend in literary Dublin: according to the wags in the pub, 'Con' was short for 'Continental', an indication of his cosmopolitan tastes instead of a mere diminutive. Or had it to do with the lettering on the face of Leventhal's parents' sweetshop, 'Con Leventhal Fectionaries'? Con was an old Paris hand who had decided to spend his last years there, near his old friend: Beckett helped him find a billet on the Avenue Montparnasse, only a stone's throw away. Con was a small, delicate, determined Dublin Jew with a lame leg, a lover of ladies and horses, and a drinker of the old school, who could keep going day and night without showing undue signs of wear.

I had already been impressed with Beckett's sense of discipline: the mornings for writing, phone calls and presumably correspondence between twelve and one, a light lunch, then afternoon meetings with Schneider or dark-avised Roger Blin; I sometimes glimpsed them conducting their theatrical business in neighbourhood cafés like the Raspail Vert. Then a few drinks with chosen confidants, *souper* with Suzanne, and so, presumably, to bed, unless his relentless insomnia was biting, and he might sally forth again; it had been late at night that I had seen him with Giacometti.

But the arrival of Con seemed to subvert all this discipline. Now, if we met, it would be Leventhal, as well as Peter Lennon (a young writer from Dublin earning his living as a cultural correspondent for *The Guardian*), or other stray Irish passing through, like Beckett's former student, Leslie Daiken, a Dublin Jew like Leventhal. It was as if, after a day as a normal French *écrivain*, Beckett was transformed into an Irish werewolf. And the dives were different – not the sombre formality of the Closerie, or the side bar of La Coupole – but the Falstaff, an old haunt of the twenties where the barman remembered Hemingway; the Rosebud, which ran until near dawn; and an even more downmarket dive called Scott's, which had the louche atmosphere of an old whorehouse. Indeed, Sam and Con seemed to know a lot about the ladies of the evening. Although the brothels were officially closed, there were still to be seen, in dim streets in Montparnasse, ladies loitering with handbags at knee level. '*Bon soir, Con!*' they murmured, as the dapper old Dubliner passed slowly by, a formal but hilarious greeting, considering the pun in French.

This was a different Beckett, the cockatoo hairdo flaring as he ran excited hands over or through it, the brandy or whiskey flowing (you could not pay for a drink in his company), the severe face crinkling with laughter. Why this dramatic transformation? It was mainly the gently subversive genius of Con, with whom Sam could discuss old Dublin days at Trinity with rueful nostalgia, what an excluded Catholic like myself would wryly regard as 'Trinners' talk. I also provided a vague link with the University College Dublin contemporaries who had been his poetic pals, people like Denis Devlin and Brian Coffey, and his best friend, Thomas MacGreevy. And Peter Lennon was from Dublin, and shared Beckett's detestation of the more oppressive aspects of the new

Irish state. When John McGahern's second book, *The Dark*, was banned, Beckett waxed indignant, convinced that our countrymen would never change in their reactionary philistinism: *Watt* had got the hammer in 1954, and *Molloy* in 1956. And when my collection of stories, *Death of a Chieftain*, got savaged by Patrick Kavanagh in an Irish periodical and I was contemplating a riposte, Beckett was emphatic: 'Don't answer them; they're not worth it!' But there was also his uneasiness at his increasing fame: after the Formentor prize that he had shared with Borges, loomed the Nobel, and in some weird way he wanted to be reassured that the home ground was still there, and liked the fellow feeling that our little Irish group provided, where local references did not have to be explained.

The exchanges between Con and Sam could be marvellously comic, like two old stand-up comedians. Late one night, Con and I were discussing love, with the leisurely wistfulness of two world-weary romantics, a conversation that clearly irritated Beckett profoundly, both intellectually and emotionally. The great head was heaving up and down, the exasperated sighs were proliferating, until Sam saw a chance to shove in his oar:

'No love,' he said with satisfaction. 'Only fuck!'

There was a startled silence, before Beckett moved in again, ignoring the shock on both our faces, especially Con's. Con might like the activity, but he rarely used bad language. 'Eat – drink – fuck,' Sam declared. 'That's all,' adapting, consciously or unconsciously, Eliot's famous lines in *Sweeney Agonistes*.

I saw Con slowly gather his wits about him, hunch his shoulders and begin gently but implacably to stalk his quarry. The dialogue between those two old friends, like an impromptu playlet, ran something like this:

CON (*playing his pal like a fish*): We've been friends for a long time, Sam.

SAM (*uneasy and puzzled*): Old friend. Oldest of friends.

C: We go a long time back.

S: Very far back.

C: Then why wouldn't you speak to me once?

S (*agitated*): Always speak to you, Con. Always. Old friend. (*Repeated vehemently.*)

C: Yet you ignored me. You refused to see me.

S: Impossible! Oldest of friends! Always recognised Con. (*In his agitation, Sam speaks in the third person about himself, and is almost babbling.*)

C: You ignored me. I came into Harcourt Street railway station, and you hid behind one of those big neo-classical pillars.

S (*startled*): Behind a pillar, Con?

C: Yes. Behind a pillar. D'you remember the pillars in Harcourt Street? D'you remember the Harcourt Street station? D'you remember the line?

As in a trance, Beckett reeled off the names of the stations, a south Dublin litany of now closed and forgotten halts: Harcourt Street, Ranelagh, Beechwood Avenue, Milltown, Churchtown, Dundrum, Carrickmines, Stillorgan, Leopardstown near his own early home, Foxrock. Con listened silently, then moved in for the kill.

C: So you know the station and you know the line?

S: Like the back of me hand. Travelled it morning and night, to and from Trinity. Leaving home, going home.

C: Yet you hid from me behind one of those Grecian pillars!

S: Behind a pillar, from you? (*His expression a study in confusion.*)

C: Yes, you hid behind a pillar in Harcourt Street railway station from me – with a woman. Yes! You, who deny love, hid from your oldest friend because you were with a woman.

Beckett was silenced, flummoxed. Then he perked up.

'You're right,' he said brightly, 'the woman from Dundrum. You also fancied her yourself. But she always got off half-way.'

While Beckett could be great company, and gravely humorous, there was no doubt that his view of the universe was gloomy, 'as bleak as the arsehole of a Siberian wolf', to quote my wife, Madeleine. So I never felt bad if I was in poor humour myself, and indeed things seemed to go better, even swimmingly, if I was despondent as well, with sometimes several minutes of sympathetic silence between our carefully phrased sentences. He kept recommending me to read Calderón's *La Vida es Sueño*, a key play for him which he almost consented to stage, and I often had the strong impression that, for him, our world was unreal, almost a dream, a cruel dream. And because it was such, the courtesies had to be observed, politeness was all, and although as an adolescent he had spurned the Spartan politeness of Foxrock, that early regime served him well now, keeping the beasts at bay.

As I got to know him, I always tried to get my own complaints in first, knowing he would easily vanquish me in the woe stakes. There was one period where I was deeply depressed, and the black dog, or the blue devil as Burns calls it, had fastened its claws on my back. My marriage was not going well, my work was not going well, and I was plagued with insomnia. Pills were not working, and I was not really into counting sheep.

'So what', I asked Sam, 'do you do, when things are not going well and you can't sleep?'

'I play the course at Carrickmines, the old and the new, all eighteen holes, one by one, in my head.'

'I can't play golf', I cried.

'That's a handicap.'

I looked up, startled. He was smiling.

Again, we were discussing suicide, a subject to which I brought all a young man's romantically gloomy ardour. Beckett, however, seemed to have given the matter a lot of thought. Although he was of the select company of those who, like Sophocles, would prefer not to have been born, when I asked him if he ever thought of ending it, he replied brusquely, 'Out of the question. But I have thought of disappearance.' His best plan, he elaborated, was a boat with a hole in the bottom, to be dredged up by divers. Then a philosophic sigh. 'That's legally impossible too. The widow wouldn't inherit for seven years.'

Another time, we were comparing ailments, a favourite topic: his eyes were beginning to cloud with cataracts, and, although he had been quite a sportsman in his youth, playing rugby and cricket for Portora and Trinity, and even boxing, his physical faculties were declining. He no longer played tennis with Suzanne or Bill Hayter, and even walked more gingerly, afraid of blundering into things. And he had suffered all his life from embarrassing ailments, a mouthful of bad teeth, boils on his bum, and now near blindness, not helped by his earlier tendency to buy non-prescription spectacles from the local chemist. But he never indulged in self-pity, describing his loss of sight as banal compared to the agony of his master, Joyce.

Athletic prowess and poor health seemed to run in the Beckett family: he startled me once by saying that he now had two uncles with only one leg between them. He said it with the grimly cheerful humour that never seemed to fail him, and alas it was true. The Becketts had circulatory problems, and Uncle Jim, a rugby captain and champion swimmer, had had both legs amputated, while his Uncle Gerald, who had played rugby for Ireland, and scored a try in a win against Scotland at Lansdowne Road, ended up with a wooden leg. Which came first, the chicken or the leg; in other words, did such miseries come to Sam's silent call? He had been a hospital orderly after the war, and always ministered without complaint to friends in adversity. And he had watched at the deathbed of both his parents and his beloved brother Frank. So there was some justification for the savagery of his humour, which recalled Alba in his first novel, *A Dream of Fair to Middling Women*, when she goes around 'grousing an old Irish air: "Woe and pain, pain and woe / Are my lot, night and noon ..."' But while Sam might have been as specialised in sadness as a keening Irish crone, one could argue that, when the microcosm of his interior misery was mirrored in the larger cataclysm of the Second World War, he was finally able to slough off his Beladqua early self and come into his own.

For the Irish male, getting drunk together seems a necessary preface to intimacy, and Sam was no exception to that national trait. One balmy 14 July, in the evening, I was sitting calmly on the terrace of the Sélect with Serge Fauchereau, a serious young French critic who was working on a study of modern American poetry. Suddenly Sam lurched by, clutching a lady, whom I recognised as Joan Mitchell, a distinguished American painter whom I had already met, and whose powerful abstracts we all admired. Sam spied me, and drew to a swaying halt at our table, grinning glassily. He was clearly already on the tear, that most un-French of rituals. (I had begun to understand, through observing my in-laws and friends, that while the French might drink more than most of us, it was to be absorbed slowly, and only immediately before, during, and directly after meals. The berserk quality of an Irish or Anglo-American bender was alien and even frightening to them.)

Nothing would do Sam but that I should accompany him. The Cricket, as Joan Mitchell kept calling my poor French friend, was also swept along, awed and astonished by our mad antics. I tried to stall our downward slide: since I already knew that Sam had a soft spot for the lady, something he kept confirming quite vigorously at the café table, why did they not move to some quiet hotel, instead of getting drunk with us on Bastille night?

'Where does one go to be alone?' cried Sam, ignoring the fact that he was surrounded by small *hotels du passage*, which must have been familiar to him in the past.

Indeed, that seemed to be the problem – his growing fear of being recognised, especially in his own *quartier*. Joan was clearly not pleased by his prevarications, and in a desperate effort to play Cupid, I suggested that they should come home with me, since Madeleine was away, and take over the studio, while I continued my evening with Serge with whom I was discussing recent poems by John Berryman, and the San Franciscans Snyder and Duncan.

But my helpful offer of a billet was brushed aside by an alcoholically ambivalent Sam, who led our tattered band in the direction of the usual watering holes, where Con and others were already lying in wait, celebrating the French national holiday in Irish fashion. Supper was scorned as the spirits cascaded, and we were all more than merry, except Joan Mitchell, who felt the evening had taken a wrong turn when Sam had sighted an Irish pal and used him as a diversion, a green herring. Joan was a famous drinker herself, so, after a few belts of Scotch, she lit into me and my French friend.

'Listen, Montague, do you always travel with your pet cricket?'

I tried to translate this for Serge, who could not quite see the connection between being a critic and a marsh-dwelling insect. It was all the more embarrassing because Serge was of small stature, although not of mind: he was the best-read Frenchman I had yet met. 'Don't you know, Montague, that critics are a low form of life, so low that they shouldn't be spoken to, only kicked in the butt? I never met a critic who knew his ass from his elbow, so there must be something wrong with you if you have to travel with a pet critic.' Sam was enjoying the conversation, while trying to limit the damage; he must have had some experience of Joan on the warpath. And Serge was grinning with pleasure, especially since I was translating only half of what was being said about him. Joan shifted her shotgun in my direction.

'Sam says that you're a poet. Do you think that you're a poet?'

I deflected this question as delicately as possible, murmuring the old Irish belief that it was an honour only others could bestow, and should not be claimed too loosely by oneself, or some such sententious sentiment.

'Okay, so Sam says you're a poet, but are you a *great* poet? I know I'm a great painter, or at least I feel so after I've finished a painting. But do you feel that you're a *great* poet?'

Sam had become visibly agitated, hurling his arms around, heaving his head, as he often did when in some distress (at a later stage he would sometimes retire totally into himself, like a mule or a mollusc). But now he seemed to be dimly aware that Joan was taking out her frustration on me with her implacable interrogation, which was all the more discomfiting because it was unfair: I understood that this was not the end to the evening that she had hoped for, but I *had* tried (twice) to assist their rendezvous. Beckett became as sober and clear as he could under the circumstances.

'It's all a question of age,' he said. 'John is still young, but I think he's working well. They only start to call you "great" when you're old, and nearing the graveyard. Before that, they don't even read you, so how would they know? It's all a matter of age, and so-called dignity: a tip of the cap to the corpse.'

The critic was delighted by this high-level literary exchange. Unaccustomed to such lethal draughts of spirits, he was moving in and out of consciousness, but his excitement at being with Beckett, and a famous painter whom he also admired, kept him almost on course. But Joan would not give up, determined to drive a wedge into the evening she had lost.

'What about Sam's poetry? Is that great poetry?'

I fielded that as well as I could. 'Well, it's a different kind of poetry from mine – more learned, more intellectual. Sam is better educated than me, went to better schools, so he knows much more. He learnt a lot from Pound and the surrealists. But since he's here, why don't you ask him yourself, as you asked me?'

She swivelled her shotgun-gaze towards Sam and repeated the question, less sharply. But after a certain point in the evening Sam did not believe in lengthy intellectual exchange, and that point had now been reached.

'My poetry,' said Sam, 'my poetry.' And he began to giggle. 'My poetry is –' But he never finished the sentence, because he was lost in a bubble of giggles, which ended in a snort of laughter, and a mangled mutter of 'My poetry ...' as his hands implored heaven. As a critical judgement it left us back at the starting post, and even Joan did not dare enquire further.

By this time we had reached the Falstaff, and dawn was beginning to break. Our exchanges, which had collapsed into listless half-sentences, were brought to a close when a large shadow fell across the door. The well-known French-Canadian painter, Jean-Paul Riopelle, Joan Mitchell's partner, had come in search of her. There were some polite murmurs of upcoming exhibitions and shows, before Jean-Paul gathered in Joan as a bear might sweep in his mate. Con suggested another drink for the road, and as dawn finally broke, we tottered out of the last dive, the former *bordel* called Scott's, with baby-pink decor. I propped Beckett along, who propped Serge, while Leventhal mooched ahead, swinging wide his lame leg.

'Con's a great man,' said Sam admiringly, watching him steer a careful but unsteady path home.

We parted ways at the top of the Boulevard Raspail, and I managed to hoist my swaying companions down as far as the Boulevard St Jacques, sometimes taking the two sides of the road with us, not to speak of the wall. But the morning traffic was still light, and I succeeded in half-carrying, half-shuffling Beckett into his home quarters, before giving him a final leg up. Then I hauled Serge along our slumbering courtyard, and deposited him on the spare bed that I had offered to the reluctant lovers only a few hours before, although now, in the soft grey light of a Paris morning, it seemed aeons ago. In later years, Serge would describe it as one of the most extraordinary nights of his life.

A day afterwards, there was a brief but beautiful note through the post: 'Thanks for your help up the blazing boulevard.'

Even my disapproving spouse was impressed.

THE CUSTOM OF THE *QUARTIER*

And I was impressed by the politeness of the inhabitants of our *quartier*, which probably attracted someone with such a deep sense of privacy. Though he drank heavily himself, Sam was disturbed by certain kinds of flamboyant 'Oirish' drunkenness, like Brendan Behan or Peter O'Toole, both of whom were prone to descend on Paris and wreck all around them, like rugby supporters. O'Toole was an especial *bête noire*, having played a large part in an Abbey production of *Godot*, which Beckett had not sanctioned. The etiquette of the *quartier* demanded that one should not intrude on other people's dialogue-in-progress. Thus, when the Irish writer Aidan Higgins and his wife passed through

Paris on their way home from Spain, I found a place for them to stay, and I acted as his interpreter, since he had little French. But I left Aidan and his wife alone with Beckett, knowing well how easily Sam could be upset by too much social pressure.

This sense of decorum was deeply rooted in French artistic life: you did not barge in as you might in a raucous Dublin pub like McDaid's. Sometimes, in the mornings, I would shoot out to the Liberté, one of the three bars at the top of the Avenue du Maine, for a late morning *café* or *calvados*, and see Sartre at a corner table. Or around three o'clock, I would glimpse him taking a late lunch at La Coupole. If I went down to the kiosk by the Rotonde in Montparnasse, to buy my *Herald Tribune*, I would sometimes see his strange, small, intent figure, one eye narrowed behind those thick glasses, eagerly rifling through his early copy of *Le Monde*. But if I had not called on Simone, despite Nelson Algren's encouragement, why should I bother Jean-Paul?

People make their paths through a city the way animals do through a field, and I had grown up to recognise the determined little ley-lines that rabbits make on their way to and from their burrows, and the field where the hares lived, growing careless only when they emerged for their spring boxing matches. And cows, even bulls, usually kept to their territory, except when love horned in. So why should humans not preserve the same instinctive courtesy? One did not intrude unless there was a genuine reason.

So when Madeleine and I found a lonely Brassaï playing the pinball machines, we spoke to him, because he had recently been injured, bewildered by a new set of traffic lights on the Boulevard Raspail, and neighbourly concern seemed in order. He confided that it was his seventieth birthday, and since he seemed totally alone, we swept him off to dinner, where he entertained us with stories of old Paris, his days with Henry Miller and the ladies of Montmartre. And in due course I went round with Hayter to see him, and admired the wonderful small sculptures he was doing then.

What was important was how the presence of the famous or gifted was taken for granted. At a lavish party given by Oonagh Guinness, mother of my friend Garech Browne, in her Paris flat, I became aware of the obsessed way in which one of the guests was gazing around him, in particular at a marvellous but strange-looking girl with a pronounced squint. 'Isn't she beautiful?' he repeated again and again. Clearly someone who disdained conventional ideals of beauty, since the young woman was surrounded by models from Oonagh's husband's *maison de couture*, tall, slender and vacuous. He looked as if he wanted to take a permanent impression of her, a kind of mental photograph. And when I asked who he was, I was told it was Man Ray.

THE BECKETT FAMILY BAND

Sam was amused by my stories about the founding of Claddagh Records, and liked Garech, whose mother he had met under one of her manifestations. And of course Luggala was one of the most beautiful parts of his beloved Wicklow. So, in due course, Garech decided that Claddagh should do a Beckett record, with the warm approval of its Speech Director (myself). We had a long-distance hope that we might lure Beckett to record something himself, a hope which Garech transferred to me, since I lived round the corner from our man. As I was gathering *The Faber Book of Irish Verse*, I had been reading Sam's poetry carefully, and could ask, with feigned innocence, how one should speak 'Alba', or my own favourite, 'Gnome'. But I got short change. I understood his hesitations, since I had great difficulty in reading my own work before an audience, and could only force myself to perform for the always necessary shekels. It raised the perennial dispute about whether the author or an actor should read the poet's work, a subject on which my poetic generation held a unanimous opinion, whereas Sam seemed to be on the side of the actor. I persevered, but his reluctance was profound, and he would offer only stage directions. It seemed to me to amount to a superstition, as though he would lose a piece of his soul if his voice were captured, the way some cultures react to being photographed.

Meanwhile, back at the Dublin ranch, Garech was trying to comply with all of Beckett's exacting demands: Con Leventhal, of course, for the sleeve note, with a drawing by Arikha of Beckett with his spectacles pushed up high on his forehead, like racing goggles. And since there was no question of him reading anything himself (though I had continued to press hard for even a fragment), we were all old friends of the actor Jack MacGowran, who was one of Beckett's favourite voices. Sam suggested a selection from his novels, because the plays had had a fair outing, but since he couldn't, wouldn't come to Dublin, Garech had to arrange a recording session in London. And though Sam had little or no appreciation of our involvement with Irish traditional music, Garech was glad to record the one and only performance of the Beckett Family Band, with cousin John on the harmonium, nephew Edward on the flute, and Sam, with mellow vigour, striking the gong, a sound he had probably heard for the first time as a young man at the Abbey Theatre.

Garech tried his sly best to conspire with our engineers to catch a whisper of Beckett's directions to Jack, but Sam was too wily a bird, making sure that all extraneous material and out-takes were destroyed, until not a murmur of him remained. From where did all this precision and exactitude come? Perhaps from some glimpse of his father's work-room, but he also had a version of, what Seán Ó Riada claimed, perfect pitch, so that the least wrong note pained him. And where his work was concerned, he was stubborn to the point of mulishness. When I was still engaged in trying to lure him into vinyl immortality, to get him to read even the most minuscule of verses, he put down his glass and smiled, switching suddenly from English to French, saying, '*Je te vois venir*': I see you coming.

After the recording had been done to his satisfaction, I saw a new aspect of Beckett, his impatience, as he harried Claddagh for the finished product. It took time, especially since we knew that any slip would anger the Master, not only the recording itself, but the reproduction of the Arikha drawing, and the splendid photograph on the cover of a vigilant Beckett with his alter ego, Jack, both listening to Beckett's words, Jack's voice. The irony was that while Beckett did not want to be recorded, Garech hated being photographed, as well as being as perfectionist as Sam in his attention to detail. So I was dealing with two Protestant fusspots, who were also like coy maidens, one refusing to speak his own words while tolerating the camera, the other averting his head from the photographer's flash while hounding down the sound of the human voice. Sam had also decided that the delay was due to Hibernian laxity, and he gave out his usual spiel about the Irish, forgetting that I was connected with the company, until I brought box after box of records back with me from Ireland. It still seems to me one of the best speech records in existence, and a key to Beckett's own sense of his prose masterwork, which would serve as an unacknowledged guide for actors in the future. I do not think, however, that the Beckett Family Band could ever have made it on the road.

THE PUBLIC MAN

Jean Martin, the French actor, said that Beckett made it a practice not to appear for his own plays, but he usually showed the flag for the Irish contribution to the Théâtre des Nations, especially by the Abbey. He attended their production, for instance, of *The Countess Cathleen*. Indeed, he brought his wife as well, which was one of the few occasions that I met this sober, quiet woman, reputed to be death on spirits and addicted to herbal remedies. Sam's introduction was brief. As Madeleine and I were making the necessary theatrical small talk with him, I enquired about the presence or absence of his own spouse.

'She's here,' he said, and no more, indicating a silent figure by his side.

Madeleine leaped the awkward gulf with a few platitudes in French, but it was clear that Sam was too shy to be adept at formal greetings. He did break through the tiresome opening night social rituals when I began to inveigh against the slow plot and predictable Twilight rhythms of the early Yeats play.

'Wait until the end,' he cautioned. 'There are some beautiful lines that nearly save the play, when Yeats lets go. And remember, it was early; I've hidden mine out of sight.'

I was about to enquire what play he was speaking of, when he surprised me by launching into a sort of sing-song, perhaps the kind of chanting he had heard from Yeats himself on the Abbey stage, when he was a student:

The years like great black oxen tread the world,
And God the herdsman goads them on behind,
And I am broken by their passing feet.

But Sam could put on a show if he had to. He came out loyally for
Jack's one-man show in a large Paris theatre, the Théâtre Édouard VII.
It was destined to fail, because neither Sam nor Jack were yet the cult
figures they would later become, and also because what we now recog-
nise as a typical Beckettian performance (one actor on an austere stage
delivering a monologue) had not yet caught on for general audiences.
Besides, it was in English, an hour and a half of fine gloomy prose, with
Jack shuffling around, swathed in a long, shabby coat, an extended
public version of our Claddagh record, I was glad to observe.

There was a well-fuelled reception afterwards, though, and, miracle
of miracles, Sam was there at the end of a receiving line, not in his polo
neck and corduroy jacket, but in a fairly swanky suit and tie, a contrast
to his down-at-heel alter ego on the stage. Considering his almost patho-
logical shyness, it was a considerable effort for him, and I watched in
admiration as he bent to speak to some of the most boring society
people in Paris. On the edge of the throng, I saw a distinguished English
lady novelist, sitting, as I thought, disconsolately. Betrayed by the general
mood of generosity, I thought she might like to meet Sam, so I led her to
the top of the queue, proud to introduce one accomplished writer to
another. I had forgotten, from previous cloudy meetings in London
literary pubs like the George, that she had a tongue like an adder.

She tore into Beckett. She had been through the war too, and had
seen people killed, but if she felt like him, she would have the decency
to keep it to herself. His writing was a disgrace to humanity. If she
despaired about people the way he seemed to, she wouldn't write at all.
He was doing the dirt on life.

It was obviously a well-rehearsed speech, and of a kind that Sam had
heard before. He did not answer, but let his head droop, like a tired horse,
and when the tirade had exhausted itself, he raised an imploring gaze.

'Where is Con?' he asked.

I hurried to fetch him, and he came to the rescue immediately. Olivia Manning was filling her glass and smirking.

'Sorry, John. I suppose you think that was bad of me, but I've wanted to do it for years, and you gave me the chance.'

I felt like shit warmed up, but Beckett never reproached me, or enquired who she was. Years later, in a biography of that amiable Oxford publisher, Dan Davin, I read how he detested Olivia Manning so much that when she died his only comment was that she had been 'poisoned, no doubt, by her own venom'. But Sam seemed to have a practised skill in dealing with those smaller sharks that cruise the literary waters, hoping to wound and feed off the larger fish. There are times I have longed for his detachment, as another scraggy failed writer injects sullen bile into what one had hoped would be a civil exchange.

SALUTE IN PASSING

In my more grandiose moments, I dreamt that I would be the young Irish writer who would carry on from these great men. But if the young Beckett was daunted by the Joyce of *Finnegans Wake* (his first public efforts in French were in that famous collaborative translation of the Anna Livia monologue), how much more difficult it would be to try to follow his trilogy as well! Besides, the great era of modern experiment seemed to be over, especially in prose. I managed a creditable book of stories, which Sam said he liked, especially the title story, an extravaganza set in the south of Mexico, 'Death of a Chieftain', because it was the most experimental. And translations of my poems were also leaking into the more prestigious journals, and getting some notice. I was reviewing, as well, for *Le Monde* and *La Quinzaine Littéraire*, usually discussing my Irish contemporaries like McGahern and the more erratic Higgins, as well as Clarke, Kavanagh and Kinsella, to create a French context for the newer Irish writing. It was almost a weakness of mine, dreaming a family to compensate for the one I had only briefly had.

But poetry, it was finally becoming clear, was my real passion. And something that had become depressingly obvious to me was that Sam no longer read much poetry, even modern French poetry. After all, he had been introduced by Rudmose Brown at Trinity to his French contemporaries, and had worked for a while on Jouve. The perfervid imagination of Jouve, his heady brew of sensuality, Catholicism and psychoanalysis, might no longer appeal to the often ascetic Beckett, but for someone of my Catholic background of incense, purity and ritual punishment, it was still fascinating. Beckett had also translated Éluard for the little magazine *This Quarter*, poems reproduced in his friend George Reavey's anthology, *Thorns of Thunder*, which I had found in the library of the Royal Dublin Society. And Char had been a Resistance leader in the Vaucluse, not far as the crow flies from Roussillon, where Beckett had found refuge: I made a kind of pilgrimage to Char at his home near the beautiful village of Isle sur la Sorgue, with its slowly turning water wheel. And squat Guillevic, ironic Frénaud, and their friend Follain, could be seen traipsing through the streets of Paris after some literary *soirée* where the wine had flowed: Follain was killed crossing a street near the Louvre.

So while Beckett's interest in modern French poetry was lapsing, I was beginning to believe that it was far more exciting and varied than anything recent in English, with its strong philosophical undertone which impressed my intellectually hungry mind. The only more recent poet Sam had translated was Alain Bosquet, which I reproached him for, since Bosquet was mainly a journalist, but Sam simply said he was a 'pal', which seemed to excuse everything. As for my own pals, Esteban, Bonnefoy, Deguy, Dupin, Fourcade, Marteau, he seemed never to have heard of them; *le bande à Beckett*, Beckett's gang, was mainly connected with the theatre and the *nouveaux romans* of Les Éditions de Minuit.

I was given a chance, however, to offer affection and homage to my great compatriot and neighbour. One must remember that the French did not fall head over heels with joy when Beckett received the Nobel, which Malraux had been expecting; Mauriac was also prone to make sour comments about this incomprehensible import. However, the *Magazine Littéraire* asked me to write a long piece on Beckett, upon which I and Madeleine slaved for a summer. So I found myself in the company of admirers like Blin and Ionesco (from the theatre), and

Alain Robbe-Grillet, Claude Mauriac and Claude Simon, briefly joining *le bande à Beckett*. Sam liked the essay himself, particularly because it also placed him in an Irish, or even a Trinity College, tradition, of Swift, Goldsmith, Berkeley and Synge, names not always bandied around the Sorbonne and Saint-Germain.

Rombaldi, the French publishing house for which Madeleine was now working, had a plan to reproduce this essay, which had covered both the Irish and French bases, in a combined French and New York English-language edition commemorating the Nobel literary prizes. But Barney Rosset of the Grove Press was dog-in-the-mangerish about this plan, which was a pity, because the French edition was handsomely produced and printed, again with drawings by Arikha. But the kind of sour nemesis which stalks great writers struck again, with a blandly hostile introduction by a member of the Swedish Academy, which made it clear that he was not a Beckett fan.

Meanwhile, inspired by my surroundings, I was trying to write in French myself, muttering lines as I marched the streets. But I was beginning to realise that it was not only Sam who had lost interest in contemporary poetry, but the whole French nation, and that this indifference to poetry might always have been a national characteristic, except during periods of crisis, as when poetry was part of the Resistance. 'Poetry is a pastime,' says Alceste in Molière's *Le Misanthrope*. And although the context is comic, it finds an echo in Baudelaire's sombre reflection, '*La France a horreur de la poésie*'. It was not part of their lives, even in the raging outcast manner of a Kavanagh, or the solemn intoning of Clarke in his weekly poetry programme on Radio Éireann. The French equivalents as public personalities, keepers of the flame, the tribal conscience, were now the prose writers, the *causeries* of Sartre, the *bloc-notes* of François Mauriac. Only Cocteau had a public face, and his poetry seemed lightweight compared to the great poets of the period, like Jouve, Char and Ponge. Prévert was also read, because he was simple, and could be sung. But my French poetic contemporaries had to be content with tiny editions of two hundred or so, mainly *service de presse*, a matter of prestige for publishing houses, unless and until they weathered indifference long enough to reach the pocket book stage.

Two later anecdotes would come to crystallise and symbolise my increasing disaffection with the French attitude towards poetry. A distinguished novelist from Brittany, Michel Mohrt, was a regular visitor to Ireland, and observing the public success of my long poem, *The Rough Field*, recommended it to his own publishing house, Gallimard. A surprised Deguy was part of the reading committee, and piled in behind the proposal, only to have it turned down by the boss himself, who picked up the book, and, discovering it was written in verse, placed it aside, declaring, '*Mais, c'est de la poésie! Ça vend pas.*'

And years later, when Deguy and other French friends had assembled my *Selected Poems* in French, it was recommended by Beckett to Lindon of Les Éditions de Minuit, which had been founded as a Resistance publishing house. Lindon turned it down for the same reason as Gallimard, his clinching argument being that even Sam's poetry didn't sell. If I was to have a future as a poet, it was clearly not going to be in France, from which I had already unconsciously begun to beat a retreat.

Based on a lecture given in Trinity College Dublin on 11 February 2000.

BIOGRAPHICAL NOTE

Born in Brooklyn, New York, in 1929, John Montague was raised in Garvaghey, County Tyrone, and educated at University College Dublin, Yale University and the University of California at Berkeley. He co-founded Claddagh Records, and became president of Poetry Ireland in 1979. His poetry includes *Forms of Exile* (1958); *Poisoned Lands* (1961); *A Chosen Light* (1967); *Tides* (1970); *The Rough Field* (1972); *A Slow Dance* (1975); *The Great Cloak* (1978); *The Dead Kingdom* (1984); *Mount Eagle* (1988); *Time in Armagh* (1993); *Collected Poems* (1995); *Smashing the Piano* (1999); *Carnac* (1999); *Drunken Sailor* (2004); *Speech Lessons* (2011); and *New Collected Poems* (2012). His *Second Childhood* was published posthumously in 2017. He won the Marten Toonder Award in 1977, a Guggenheim fellowship in 1980, the Ireland Funds Literary Award in 1995, the Lifetime Achievement Irish Book Award 2016; he was made a Chevalier de la Légion d'Honneur in 2010 and has honorary doctorates from SUNY, the Sorbonne, UCD, Ulster University at Coleraine and UCC. He was Ireland Professor of Poetry from 1998–2001. John Montague died in Nice in December 2016.

ACKNOWLEDGEMENTS

The author and the publisher gratefully acknowledge the following for permission to reprint copyrighted material. Every effort has been made to seek copyright clearance on referenced text. If there are any omissions, UCD Press will be pleased to insert the appropriate acknowledgement in any subsequent printing or editions.

Claude Esteban: 'And Maybe All Was Written', translated by John Montague, from *A Smile between the Stones/Sur la Dernière Lande* (Agenda Editions, 2008). Reprinted by kind permission of Agenda Editions.

John Montague: 'Salute, in Passing, for Sam', 'The Sean Bhean Bhocht', and 'Sunset', from *Collected Poems* (The Gallery Press, 1995). Reprinted by kind permission of the Estate of John Montague and The Gallery Press.

Nuala Ní Dhomhnaill: 'Blodewedd', translated by John Montague, from *Pharaoh's Daughter* (The Gallery Press, 1990). Reprinted by kind permission of The Gallery Press.

Cathal Ó Searcaigh: 'Clabber: The Poet at Three Years', translated by John Montague, from Montague, *Drunken Sailor* (The Gallery Press, 2004). Reprinted by kind permission of The Gallery Press.

BIBLIOGRAPHY

Samuel Beckett: *A Dream of Fair to Middling Women* (Arcade Classics, 2012).

John Davidson: 'The Runnable Stag', from *Holiday and Other Poems* (E. Grant Richards, 1906).

Michael Davitt: 'Seimeing Soir', translated by John Montague, from *Irish Pages* 3:1 (spring/summer 2005).

Michel Deguy: *Comme si, Comme ça: Poèmes 1980–2007* (Poésie/ Gallimard, 2012); and 'Royal Song', translated by John Montague, from *Modern Poetry in Translation* 16 (1973).

T. S. Eliot: *The Waste Land* (Faber, 2013).

Claude Esteban: 'And Maybe All Was Written', translated by John Montague, from *A Smile between the Stones/Sur la Dernière Lande* (Agenda Editions, 2008); 'A Horizontal Sky', translated by John Montague, from *Atlantis* 3 (1971).

Robert Graves: 'The Portrait', from *Poems Selected by Himself* (Penguin, 1966).

Ted Hughes: 'Out', from *New Selected Poems, 1957–1994* (Faber and Faber, 1995).

James Joyce quoted in Richard Ellmann: *James Joyce* (Oxford University Press, 1959).

John Keats: 'Ode to a Nightingale', from *Selected Poems* (William Collins, 2014).

Hugh MacDiarmid: 'Poetry and Propaganda', from *The Collected Poems: Volume One*, edited by Michael Grieve and W. R. Aitken (Carcanet, 1993).

Louis MacNeice: 'Prayer before Birth', from *The Collected Poems of Louis MacNeice*, edited by E. R. Dodds (Faber and Faber, 1966).

W. F. Marshall: 'Me an' Me Da', from *Irish Poetry: An Interpretive Anthology from before Swift to Yeats and after*, edited by W. J. Mc Cormack (NYU Press, 2000).

Robert Marteau: 'Memorial', translated by John Montague, from *Exile* 1 (1972).

Czeslaw Milosz: *The Witness of Poetry* (Harvard University Press, 1983).

John Milton: *Paradise Lost* (Penguin Classics, 2003).

John Montague: 'Salute, in Passing, for Sam', 'The Sean Bhean Bhocht', and 'Sunset', from *Collected Poems* (The Gallery Press, 1995).

Nuala Ní Dhomhnaill: 'Blodewedd', translated by John Montague, from *Pharaoh's Daughter* (The Gallery Press, 1990).

Alfred Noyes: 'The Highwayman', from *Collected Poems* (J. B. Lippincott, 1947).

Cathal Ó Searcaigh: 'Clabber: The Poet at Three Years', translated by John Montague, from Montague, *Drunken Sailor* (The Gallery Press, 2004).

Ezra Pound: *The Cantos of Ezra Pound* (New Directions, 1970).

Percy Bysshe Shelley: 'To a Skylark', from *The Poems of Shelley: Volume Three: 1819– 1820*, edited by Jack Donovan, Cian Duffy, Kelvin Everest and Michael Rossington (Routledge, 2014).

Paul Valéry: 'Complete Poem', translated by Stephen Romer, from *Twentieth Century French Poems* (Faber, 2002).

AFTERWORD

ON THE FOUNDATION OF THE IRELAND CHAIR OF POETRY

The award of the Nobel Prize for Literature to Seamus Heaney in 1995 was greeted with enormous pleasure throughout Ireland and not least by both Arts Councils, each regarding him as their own, a distinguished northerner, resident in Dublin. All those who knew him combine enjoyment of and respect for his work with respect for and enjoyment of the man himself, generous as he is with his time and his talents.

There was a widespread feeling that this honour should be marked in some permanent way. That a small island such as ours with a population of five million people should have produced three previous Nobel Prize winners, W. B. Yeats, George Bernard Shaw and Samuel Beckett, alongside James Joyce and Oscar Wilde and a chorus of distinguished peers, was surely an extraordinary achievement necessary of celebration. But how to make it a permanent celebration?

Seamus would be the first to say that he did not stand alone but was 'true brother of a company' of poets, 'mighty word' as he has said himself. Indeed, I had been fond of remarking myself, as Arts Council Chairman, that if there were a poet's world cup, an Irish or northern Irish first eleven would easily carry off the laurels.

What to do was discussed at a luncheon during the Wexford Opera Festival of 1995 by friends there gathered. It was Jean Kennedy Smith, then American Ambassador to Ireland, who said, 'What about a Chair?' No sooner said than this did indeed seem to be the best objective.

Perhaps surprisingly, there has not been, until now, a Chair of Poetry in Ireland, despite our standing in that field. It was clear we did not want a full-time academic Chair. Such an institution would lack freshness for those who were already academics and also debar many distinguished poets who are not academics from selection. We looked to the Oxford Chair of Poetry as a model, principally honorific but with the duty to give a few lectures a year and some presence in the university.

I felt our Chair could be doubly unique if it could be held jointly between universities on either side of the border, a step manifestly appropriate in timing and in principle, as recognising the universality of learning.

Given that poetry has tended to be an ill-paid profession, we did determine that the Chair should have a not wholly insignificant honorarium.

The choice of universities was obviously important and dependent on their agreement. Discussions led to the proposal of Trinity College Dublin, Queen's University Belfast, and University College Dublin. These proposals were unanimously endorsed by the joint meeting of the Arts of Northern Ireland and An Chomhairle Ealaíon in Belfast in November in 1995. We were delighted when all three universities enthusiastically accepted the invitation to participate.

There remained much to do. To co-ordinate the workings of five institutions and their own internal rules and disciplines is no light matter. But with goodwill on all sides agreement was reached on all issues. These included the name – The Ireland Chair of Poetry – and that the tenure would be three years, with the incumbent hosted by each of the three universities in turn while Ireland Professor of Poetry.

In early 1998 we sought, by way of newspaper advertisements, suggestions from the public for the first holder of the post. Each of the five sponsoring institutions prepared a short list of nominees, having considered carefully the suggestions. All five institutions were able to consult distinguished poets, critics and persons interested in the arts in arriving at their views.

The final selection was made on behalf of The Ireland Chair of Poetry Trust by Professor Seamus Heaney, Professor Andrew Mayes, Vice-Provost of Trinity, Professor Robert Cormack, Pro Vice-Chancellor of Queen's, Professor Fergus D'Arcy, Dean of the Faculty of Arts at

University College, Dublin, Professor Ciarán Benson of An Chomhairle Ealaíon and my unprofessing self. It was subsequently ratified by all five institutions.

We were delighted when John Montague accepted our invitation to become the first holder of the Chair. His body of work marked him out as a poet of the first rank. He was a critic and prose writer of achievement. He was of the island as a whole and of its exiles. It is a pleasure to applaud the distinction and dedication with which he fulfilled the duties of the office.

The chair will be enabled to publish and to reach out to the public as a result of a generous donation from Mr William D. Walsh of California, through the Ireland Funds, chaired by Sir Anthony O'Reilly. I express my keen thanks to them and to Ms Belinda Conlan, Administrator of the Chair, to Dr Maurice Hayes and to Mr John B. McGuckian for their support.

May John prove the first of many Ireland Professors of Poetry.

Donnell Deeny QC, SC
Chairman of the Trust

This Afterword was originally published in John Montague's *The Bag Apron* or *The Poet and his Community* (Lagan Press, 2001).

[67]